Eyes of Democracy

The Media and Elections

Manoah Esipisu and Isaac E Khaguli

Commonwealth Secretariat

Commonwealth Secretariat
Marlborough House, Pall Mall
London SW1Y 5HX
United Kingdom

Published by the Commonwealth Secretariat
Edited by editors4change Ltd
Designed by Wayzgoose
Cover design by Tattersall Hammarling & Silk
Index by Indexing Specialists (UK) Ltd
Printed by Hobbs the Printers Ltd, Totton, Hampshire

Views and opinions expressed in this publication are
the responsibility of the authors and should in no way be attributed
to the institutions to which they are affiliated or
to the Commonwealth Secretariat.

Wherever possible, the Commonwealth Secretariat uses paper
sourced from sustainable forests or from sources that minimise a
destructive impact on the environment.

Cover photo credit: Rebecca Nduku

Copies of this publication may be obtained from
The Publications Section
Commonwealth Secretariat
Marlborough House, Pall Mall
London SW1Y 5HX
United Kingdom
Tel: +44 (0)20 7747 6534
Fax: +44 (0)20 7839 9081
Email: publications@commonwealth.int
Web: www.thecommonwealth.org/publications

A catalogue record for this publication is available from the British Library.

ISBN: 978-0-85092-898-3 (paperback)
ISBN: 978-1-84859-031-1 (downloadable e-book)

About the Authors

Manoah Esipisu is deputy spokesperson at the Commonwealth Secretariat in London. He joined the Secretariat in September 2006 after 16 years as a correspondent at Reuters, the global news and information group, where he specialised in Africa and emerging markets issues. He also taught economics journalism, trade and covering elections for the Reuters Foundation and pioneered the post-graduate Financial Journalism programme at the University of the Witwatersrand (Wits) in Johannesburg. Esipisu's MA thesis (at Wits) focused on democratisation in Zambia, centring on the landmark 2001 elections. He is an alumnus of the Africa Leadership Programme of Marquette University's Les Aspin Centre for Government in Washington DC.

Isaac E Khaguli is a lecturer in digital and new media at the Journalism and Media Studies programme at Wits University and an online editor at Thomson Reuters SA Johannesburg bureau. He has trained journalists for organisations that include the Southern Africa Media Training Trust (NSJ) and is a frequent speaker at Highway Africa – the African continent's premier new media conference in Grahamstown. Khaguli was due to be awarded a PhD degree in Media Studies from the University of the Witwatersrand in 2009.

Acknowledgements

First I would like to thank journalists Daniel Nyirenda (Malawi), Joyce Mulama (Kenya), Timothy Selemani (Kingdom of Swaziland), Irene !Hoaes (Namibia), Anthony Everett Fraser (Trinidad and Tobago), Milton Walker (Jamaica) and Makereta Komai (Fiji), who agreed with enthusiasm to reflect on practices and experiences of covering elections in their own countries – reflections that convinced me a project such as this book was necessary. The journalists Shapi Shacinda (Zambia), Ibrahim Seibure (Sierra Leone), Lester Ifill (Barbados), Kaymar Angeline Jordan (Barbados), Sanjay Suri (India) and Nicola Mawson (South Africa) also shared their ideas on covering elections and I am grateful to them.

I am indebted to Professor Nixon Kariithi of the University of the Witwatersrand in South Africa, a long time associate with whom I share a passion to improve Africa's media in particular, who diligently edited the first raw manuscript, suggested some vital improvements and encouraged us to complete the project.

I should like to thank the Commonwealth Secretariat – particularly the Democracy Section of the Political Affairs Division – which made available the reports of Commonwealth Observer Groups to various elections in member countries. These reports are important to the extent that they offer details of real practices and offer possible remedies. Observers themselves are eminent people from all walks of life, but they are supported by a Commonwealth staff team and I'd like to thank specifically the media staff team, who are largely responsible for the media chapters that are reproduced in this book. The Head of the Democracy Section in the Commonwealth Secretariat's Political Affairs Division, Mark Stevens, provided invaluable support in shaping this book.

I am grateful to Eduardo del Buey, Communications and Public Affairs Director at the Commonwealth Secretariat, who has allowed me to freely express myself in my quest to service media partners wherever they are, and this book is one result of this – an attempt to make available to media colleagues a resource they can refer to when dealing with covering a contentions subject like elections. I am also grateful to Guy Bentham, Publications Manager at the Secretariat, who offered sound advice and constructive criticism that has brought this work this far.

My wife Waithiegeni Kanguru-Esipisu, a wonderful, devoted partner and the pillar around which my life revolves, has encouraged me to work to deliver this project.

Manoah Esipisu
London

Contents

'Elections define democracy while the media enlightens and sustains it'.

Peter Forau
Pacific Islands Forum, Suva, Fiji Islands
13 April 2006

Foreword

I am pleased to introduce a timely publication about two things that are central to the Commonwealth's vision of democratic society: good elections and good media.

Elections are the fulcrum of democracy. They are the most obvious manifestation of the fact that citizens can have a say in how they are governed, and that they can exercise a sacred right by casting a vote.

The media, meanwhile, holds up a mirror to society. It informs, it educates, it entertains. A free, lively and responsible media is a prerequisite for a functioning democracy, as much at election times as in between.

Good elections and good media are not things apart: they are intertwined. Manoah Esipisu and Isaac E Khaguli have skilfully brought the two strands together, with the simple and powerful thesis that the media can and should have a major and a responsible role in bringing about the success of an election.

The Commonwealth has long been engaged in the fields of both elections and the media. We observe elections, and where we have to be critical, we are so. Yet in the spirit of an organisation that seeks to build up its members, we then commit to making electoral systems work better, for instance through the better functioning of electoral commissions and voter registration systems.

Similarly, we support the media, and have run training courses across five continents in best journalistic ethics and practice. A successful feature of recent years has been our media training workshops in the margins of ministerial meetings, designed to strengthen the role that journalists and broadcasters can play in informing citizens about the development challenges which their own societies face.

In the last decade, the Commonwealth has gone further and combined the two fields, by including journalists in its election observer groups and by analysing the role of the media in those elections.

Some of these findings are presented in this book, including the ones in which our comments were controversial: we have been forthright but objective when we have reported on editorial bias, and on the imbalances we found in the financing and content of advertising. We will continue to ensure that our opinions on the role of the media in election processes are heard.

The media may take an election by surprise, but an election should never surprise the media. Its task is to be informed, to be prepared, to be investigative and to be ready and willing to look beyond headlines and into the meat of articles and interviews which probe the issues of democracy – fully and fairly. Electorates – and elections – depend on it. In this respect, the media is the guardian of democracy.

Kamalesh Sharma
Commonwealth Secretary-General
London, January 2009

Abbreviations

AU	African Union
BBC	British Broadcasting Corporation
CODEO	Coalition of Domestic Election Observers
COMESA	Common Market for East and Southern Africa
COG	Commonwealth Observer Group
ECK	Electoral Commission of Kenya
ECZ	Electoral Commission of Zambia
EU	European Union
GRTS	The Gambia Radio and Television Services
GECOM	Guyana Elections Commission
ICASA	Independent Communications Authority of South Africa
IEC	Independent Elections Commission
IMPCS	Institute of Media, Policy and Civil Society
IRIN	Integrated Regional Information Networks (the UN news agency)
International IDEA	International Institute for Democracy and Electoral Assistance
MBC	Malawi Broadcasting Corporation
MEC	Malawi Electoral Commission
MISA	Media Institute of Southern Africa
MMPZ	Media Monitoring Project Zimbabwe
MMU	Media Monitoring Unit (Guyana
MDC	Movement for Democratic Change (Zimbawe)
NGO	Non-governmental organisation
SABC	South African Broadcasting Corporation
SADC	Southern Africa Development Community
SMS	Short message service (text)
UNDP	United Nations Development Programme
UNESCO	UN Educational, Scientific and Cultural Organization
ZBC	Zimbabwe Broadcasting Corporation
ZEC	Zimbabwe Electoral Commission

Introduction

To declare an election successful, it must be credible. To achieve credibility, an election must meet international standards, which promote democracy and enhance security and stability.

The election must be based on a reasonable legal framework, which outlines the rules that govern the process. There must be freedom of association of political parties and other stakeholders, which in turn guarantees a competitive election on the basis of universal suffrage in which women, men and youth participate. In addition, there must be freedom of expression, which enables reasonable access to the media, and freedom of movement and assembly, so that political parties and their supporters can campaign freely. Voters also need to be free to express their will via secret ballot, and finally there must be effective legal remedy, which provides faith that the judiciary is an independent arbiter. These critical elements are covered in Articles 19 to 21 and Article 25 of the Universal Declaration on Human Rights.

There are two other conditions that are often contentious: first, that there should be a conducive environment in terms of human rights, and second, that the process needs to be transparent and accountable in order to increase confidence in the conduct of the election.

Newsrooms around the world often say that such conditions should deliver a 'free and fair' election, a phraseology that politicians also use. However, international observer groups have moved away from the 'free and fair' catch phrase, which they see as having become too simplistic. Instead they call an election either 'credible' or 'not credible'.

As one international expert on elections put it,[1]

> To reduce an election to a simple issue of free and fair doesn't do justice to the process, which is far more complex than that. Phraseology such as 'free and fair' or 'representing the will of the people' was largely abandoned by international observers a decade ago.

Covering elections presents a big challenge to the media, especially in developing countries where the average age in the newsroom[2] has dropped significantly. Tight deadlines, knowledge of relevant legislation, the political players and process, adherence

'Covering elections poses one of the most serious challenges to journalists and one of the most exciting times for journalists'.

Daniel Nyirenda
News Editor,
Daily Times, Malawi

to basic ethics and increasingly questions of personal safety all pile pressure on the media.

This book offers the media some ammunition to help deal with this challenge. Journalists in developing countries will find it a particularly useful guide. Our intention is to enable the media to use all tools at their disposal to report an election well, to realise that the coverage of an election is a skill that one should try to master and in doing so promote the democratic process in which citizens can expect balanced information regarding the process and players.

All references to 'media' in this book are in terms of the clear definition at http://www.techterms.com/definition/media[3] thus:

> ... *various means of communication. For example, television, radio and the newspaper are different types of media. The term can also be used as a collective noun for the press or news reporting agencies.*

To this definition we add the Internet, as increasingly the three mediums mentioned have online versions.

The book seeks to build on previous work in this area, such as *Media and Elections: an elections reporting handbook* by Institute of Media, Policy and Civil Society (IMPACS) Associate Ross Howard; *Free and fair: a journalist's guide to improved election reporting in emerging democracies* (Lisa Schnellinger); *Elections Reporting Handbook* (International Federation of Journalists); International Standards for the Media: briefing notes on basic principles of journalism (Article 19, Index for Free Expression, Reuters Foundation, and United Nations Education, Scientific and Cultural Organisation); *Compendium of International Standards for Elections* (European Commission); *Handbook for European Union Election Observation* (European Union); and the reports of Commonwealth Observer Groups (COGs).

The combination of existing, revised or new literature, personal experiences and reports of Commonwealth Observer Groups should provide the media with a solid comparative overview of what is needed to cover an election successfully. The reports of Commonwealth Observer Groups are of particular significance, because they relate experiences in the field. From these, media can determine how they would have reacted had they been in the same position – thereby strategically positioning themselves for when they have to tackle another election.

Following on from this introduction, the book is divided into six chapters. Chapters 1 and 2 put the role of the media in context and outline its role as a sustainer of democracy. Chapter 3 examines significant issues in reporting an election. Chapter 4 deals with technology and innovation and how these have changed the electoral landscape. Chapter 5 examines the guiding principles, such as standards and codes of conduct, while chapter 6 offers a conclusion. At the end of chapters 1–5 there are one or two testimonies from journalists who have covered an election, providing perspectives from their respective countries. These chapters are also illustrated by segments taken from various reports of Commonwealth Observer Groups which, although mild in tone, provide an important pointer to the issues the media must face during elections.

1 How the Media Enlightens and Sustains Democracy

Right to Freedom of Opinion and Expression

Article 19 of the Universal Declaration on Human Rights is the base upon which the media builds its role to enlighten and sustain democracy. This article provides that everyone has the right to freedom of opinion and expression, which includes freedom to hold opinions without interference and to seek, receive and impart information and ideas through any media and regardless of frontiers.

Regional organisations reaffirm this media role. The African Union, Organization of American States, Pacific Islands Forum, Association of Southeast Asian Nations and the European Union all make clear allegiances to a free media as a key ally in promoting democracy and a necessary element in the electoral process. The European Union and the Commonwealth Secretariat also list the media as one of the key areas to be examined when their election observer missions are deployed in any country.

In a 1971 declaration in Singapore, which was reaffirmed at their summit in Harare in 1991, the Commonwealth Heads of Government Meeting (CHOGM) committed to a series of principles to foster and sustain democracy. Among these was the declaration:

> We believe in the liberty of the individual, in equal rights for all citizens regardless of race, colour, creed or political belief, and in their inalienable right to participate by means of free and democratic political processes in framing the society in which they live. We therefore strive to promote in each of our countries those representative institutions and guarantees for personal freedom under the law that are our common heritage.[4]

A meeting of editors convened by the Commonwealth Broadcasting Association and the Commonwealth Secretariat in Canada in 2001 and a separate seminar of political editors convened by the Commonwealth Secretariat in Uganda in 2007 agreed that 'Free and democratic political processes' ultimately included elections whose credibility could not be doubted by any voter, candidate or observer. The editors noted that delivery of such credibility was very much in the hands of the media.[5]

In its *Handbook for European Union Election Observation* (2008), the European Commission puts this in context:

> *In order to ensure the full enjoyment of rights protected by Article 25 (of the Universal Declaration of Human Rights), the free communication of information and ideas about public and political issues between citizens, candidates and elected representatives is essential. This implies a free press and other media able to comment on public issues without prior censorship or restraint that informs public opinion.*[6]

The handbook also poses significant questions for European Observer Missions in terms of the media environment:

- Does the legal framework guarantee the freedom of the media? If so, is this freedom respected in practice?

- Is the media able to work freely and operate without prior censorship (including self censorship), intimidation, obstruction and interference?

- Has there been any violence against journalists? If so, does it appear election-related?

- Have any media outlets been closed as a result of government action? If so, what were the circumstances and do these appear politically motivated?

- Have any media outlets been harassed by government agencies (e.g. tax audits)

- Is libel a criminal offence? If so, have any journalists faced any criminal sanctions for their reporting? Were any such cases election-related?[7]

In *Media and Elections: an elections reporting handbook*, Ross Howard argues that the media is the most important way people find out about an election and political choices. To do this, Howard argues that the media needs to be free to report fairly on campaigns of all political parties, so people can determine if there are differences between them. Howard argues further that the media: needs to provide all people with the same information on how to vote; needs to have the freedom to ask tough questions and get answers about the transparency of an election; and needs to tell voters if there is something wrong so that it can be fixed.

In addition to these elements raised by Howard, is the media's traditional 'watch dog' role. For people to make good decisions on whom to vote for, they require information about the records of political parties and politicians individually. They require information on whether the party or parties in government delivered on their last election promises or whether they fell short; likewise, how did individual politicians perform? People also need to know how opposition parties have fared.

Informing Citizens

People also require information on current promises by parties in government, as well as those bidding to enter government at the next election. This is where media comes in – to inform citizens and to hold governments to account (and by extension, government agencies such as security agencies and civil servants).

Ace Encyclopaedia,[8] part of the Ace Electoral Knowledge Network, sees the media playing a more specific part in enabling full public participation in elections, not only by reporting on the performance of government, but also in the following ways:

- Educating the voters on how to exercise their democratic rights

- Reporting on the development of an election campaign

- Providing a platform for the political parties to communicate their message to the electorate

- Allowing the parties to debate with one another

- Reporting results and monitoring vote counting

- Scrutinising the electoral process itself in order to evaluate its fairness, efficiency and probity[9]

Taking this into account, it is evident that the media plays an indispensable role in a properly functioning democracy, specifically in setting the agenda for a successful election. Having established the important place of the media in covering elections and in the general process of oiling a functional democracy, we have to reaffirm that with this role comes great responsibility. In recognising this, the *Handbook for European Union Election Observation* states that the right to freedom of expression may come with some restrictions that must be provided for by law (i.e. such restrictions cannot be arbitrary), essentially to protect the right or reputations of others or for the protection of national security, public order, public health or morals. *The Danish Democracy Canon* (2008),[10] published by Denmark's Ministry of Education, summarises this discussion powerfully.

> *On the one hand, mass media represent a dramatic expansion of democracy. Everyone can, from one moment to the next, inform themselves about events near and far; not just about what is happening locally, but about what is happening throughout the country and in other countries. And when politicians appear on the news and give interviews, one gets a feeling of knowing them far better than if one saw them live in person once a year – if at all. Mass media can ask pointed questions on behalf of the voters, and they can deliver effective arguments in defence of fundamental freedoms. Through its mass media, a society learns something about itself each day. Mass media are not democracy's enemy, but its best friend and guarantor.*

We have made the case that media is a crucial player in electoral processes, with the twin tasks of disseminating information and keeping political and government structures accountable. We will now turn, in the next chapter, to the historical context of media in the reporting of elections.

TESTIMONY

Daniel Nyirenda – Malawi

In Malawi, covering elections poses one of the most serious challenges to journalists and is one of the most exciting times for journalists.

Elections in Malawi are governed by a 1993 constitution, framed to usher in pluralist democracy after 30 years of dictatorship. It provides for presidential, parliamentary and local government elections. The Malawi Electoral Commission (MEC) is the official body that organises elections in the country. Since 1994, when the first multiparty election was held, the country has had a total of three general elections i.e. presidential and parliamentary elections, one in May 1994, the second in May 1999 and the third in May 2004.

In terms of pre-election coverage, the practice involves covering events largely in accordance with the electoral calendar. This period starts from the day the incumbent president dissolves parliament, through the campaign period, to the actual day of polling. The period spans about four months. This period involves covering electoral candidates, both parliamentary and presidential. The media is also actively involved in covering activities of the MEC and electoral stakeholders, including donors. Some press reports also tackle registration of voters, registration of candidates, electoral malpractices, activities of electoral monitors, local and international observers and coverage of party manifestos and the candidates' campaign trail. In addition, coverage involves reporting on opinion polls by private institutions and NGOs.

In particular, there are certain issues that have pervaded all three general elections in the country – maybe with the slight exception of the 1994 general elections, which were the freest and fairest to date. For instance, in both the 1999 and 2004 general elections, the Malawi media reported on petitions by opposition presidential candidates to the MEC alleging rigging tactics and propaganda by the then ruling United Democratic Front (UDF) party and its coalition partners using public radio and television.

This election period was also characterised by coverage of the court. The most notable litigation in 2004, which was widely covered by the press, was a petition by an opposition coalition called Mgwirizano to the High Court over a shortened period between the verification of the electoral roll and polling day. Mgwirizano also lodged a complaint about abuse of resources by the ruling UDF, National Congress for Democracy

(NCD) and Alliance for Democracy (AFORD) coalition, offences which are against the country's electoral laws. In addition, the opposition queried why the MEC printed 7 million ballot papers against 5.7 million registered voters and a projection of 5 million adults (those above 18 years of age) by the National Statistical Office (NSO). Among some of the demands, the opposition wanted the courts to push forward the date for conducting the polls and for extra ballot papers to be in the custody of the court. The court shifted the date of the elections, but ruled that the ballot papers should remain in MEC custody.

During the pre-election period, the press in Malawi also reports on press briefings by and activities of observers, namely the African Union (AU), the Southern Africa Development Community (SADC), the Common Market for East and Southern Africa (COMESA) and the United Nations Development Programme (UNDP).

Election reporting

The election-reporting period covers the time between the actual polling up to the day the election results are announced. In Malawi, the constitution stipulates the polling day, unless otherwise amended by parliament. Section 67 of the constitution says:

> *The National Assembly shall stand dissolved on the 20th March in the fifth year after its election, and the polling day for the general elections for the next National Assembly shall be Tuesday in the third week of May after that year.*

On the polling day, the press covers the polling by all presidential candidates at their polling stations. Coverage also involves reporting on electoral irregularities, vote counting and analysis of unofficial results, and general observance of electoral rules by participating candidates. Issues that dominate this period in Malawi are usually delays in opening polling centres in some areas, ensuring that voters whose names do not appear on the register are barred from voting in what is known as 'ghost voting', electoral violence, forms of ballot rigging such as illegally stuffing ballot boxes and voting patterns across the country. An example of coverage during this period is a story that *The Daily Times* carried on 21 May 2004, in which marked ballot papers were found in MEC vehicles at Area 24 in the country's capital, Lilongwe. There were also cases of violence reported after the Mgwirizano coalition presidential candidate declared himself winner of the polls. To date this has been the most tasking period for journalists in Malawi.

Post-election period

The post-election period is another interesting and dramatic period in coverage of elections, as it is characterised by reactions to the poll results by winners and losers.

In Malawi, the media reports on the official election results, continues to report on any electoral irregularities during the elections and covers reactions by political parties to the poll outcome. It also reports on election results by international and local observers, litigation by losers challenging poll results, analyses of poll results by political analysts and other independent academics, views from citizens and electoral violence. In addition, this period is interesting as the media covers political deals made by the opposition and winning parties and manoeuvres among parties for key positions in the National Assembly, including that of speaker.

In between elections, the press covers, for example, by-elections, reforms and strategic plans at the MEC. Some of the processes that have taken place in the MEC since the last election are re-demarcation of constituency boundaries, restructuring of the organisation, whereby some senior officials were fired due to financial fraud during elections, and capacity building of staff.

One of the main challenges for journalists in Malawi in covering elections is intimidation and violence by political parties. Much as most politicians look for unlimited coverage during this period, those same politicians (and their supporters) are also at their weakest point, psychologically, during this time and may intimidate or become violent with reporters for doing their work.

Another serious challenge for journalists is lack of resources. The majority of journalists in Malawi live in the country's three cities, which are headquarters of the country's three regions. Because of inadequate resources they are unable to travel independently to rural areas to investigate not only stories to do with elections, but other stories as well. As a result, some journalists travel to rural areas in vehicles belonging to politicians or political parties, which obviously influences them in their writing. At the same time, communication facilities for use by reporters are usually lacking or absent in rural areas (few are able to carry laptop computers with them), so they are unable to file stories to their newsrooms while travelling in rural locations. Another challenge is that the MEC and government officials are often elusive when it comes to giving out information on elections during this period.[11]

Commonwealth Observer Group report

Zimbabwe Election,[12] 2000

Note: *The 2000 Zimbabwe election pitted the ruling Zimbabwe African National Union (ZANU-PF) of incumbent President Robert Mugabe against the opposition Movement for Democratic Change (MDC) of former trade unionist Morgan Tsvangirai. The MDC's was the first serious challenge in an election to ZANU-PF since the southern African country gained independence from Britain in 1980. The election came only a few months after the MDC successfully led opposition to a move by President Mugabe to change Zimbabwe's constitution to entrench more power in the presidency.*

The broadcast media

This is dominated by the state-owned Zimbabwe Broadcasting Corporation (ZBC) which, by law, is the sole radio and television broadcaster in the country. Under the terms of the Broadcasting Act 1996, the ZBC is a corporate body controlled by a Board appointed by the Minister of Information, Posts and Telecommunications. The mission statement of Zimbabwe Broadcasting Corporation states that it is to provide its audience with reliable information on television, radio and new media. There is no independent broadcasting regulatory authority. ...

Under the Radio Communications Act, the Posts and Telecommunications Corporation regulates, controls and supervises radio stations and radio communication services in Zimbabwe. There are an estimated one million radio sets in the country and radio is the main source of news, particularly in the rural areas. All ZBC's radio channels are broadcast to the whole country. Radio 1 is an FM station broadcasting in English. Radio 2 carries programming on FM and short wave in Shona and Ndebele. Radio 3 is an FM station broadcasting mainly music. It also has hourly news summaries and a recent survey indicated that it has an exceptionally large audience. Radio 4 is an FM and short-wave station which carries mainly educational and development programmes.

The observer group found the radio and television broadcasts of Zimbabwe Broadcasting Corporation, particularly the news bulletins, to be heavily biased in favour of the ruling party. It has been instrumental in getting the party's message to the rural areas and in denouncing the opposition. Numerous bulletins on ZBC during the election campaign started with lengthy reports of speeches by ZANU PF ministers and candidates. Sometimes such reports comprised half of the entire bulletin, which also contained no mention of any opposition parties.

Every morning, after the 7am bulletin, ZBC ran a programme presented by a police officer who detailed police reports on campaign incidents and violence. We investigated one report

> The observer group found the radio and television broadcasts of Zimbabwe Broadcasting Corporation, particularly the news bulletins, to be heavily biased in favour of the ruling party. It has been instrumental in getting the party's message to the rural areas and in denouncing the opposition. Numerous bulletins on ZBC during the election campaign started with lengthy reports of speeches by ZANU PF ministers and candidates. Sometimes such reports comprised half of the entire bulletin, which also contained no mention of any opposition parties.
>
> Commonwealth Observer Group report, Zimbabwe, 2000

presented on this programme in which the officer had stated that a farmer had sustained injuries from falling off his motorcycle. The police claimed that the war veterans on his farm had assisted him after this fall. However, the farmer said the injuries, which were serious, were the result of a heavy beating from the war veterans following an exchange of words. This was also the report carried by the independent media. This investigation cast doubt on the credibility of this daily report presented by the police to the nation.

Shortly after the arrival of the group, ZBC sent us a copy of a letter which they had sent to political parties inviting them to come to their studios and record programmes. This programming was to consist of:

- Free five-minute radio and television addresses to the nation in Shona, Ndebele and English. In these addresses the parties would explain their election manifestos. The broadcast times of these addresses was to be at ZBC's discretion.

- Free ten-minute radio interviews in which the parties would be interviewed in their election manifestos.

- Free 30-minute television interviews on the party's manifesto.

The station ran half-hour television interviews with seven party leaders in the fortnight prior to the election and provided a five-minute slot to each party to describe its manifesto. There was no code of conduct for the interviews and discussion programmes. Some observers noted that during discussion programmes the interviewers tended to allow the ruling party more time to explain their views than the opposition and to interject while the opposition participants were talking.

There were no guidelines for political party advertising and ZBC did not broadcast advertisements by the main opposition parties. The MDC had submitted some but these were not broadcast because ZBC said they needed clearance. In such cases there is no method for recourse.

Moves to end ZBC's monopoly in the media

A private company, Capitol Radio Pvt, has been trying to get a licence to start an adult contemporary music based radio station for four years. In the run up to the election, it applied to the Supreme Court to try to hear its application on an urgent basis. This was rejected and the application will possibly be heard in September.

Two weeks before the elections a new radio station, Voice of the People, started broadcasting for two hours a day in Shona, Ndebele and English on short wave across the country. Voice of the People describes itself as a community station that aims to cover contemporary issues for the average man on the street. It broadcast programmes about the elections and aimed to provide voter education and highlight issues facing the electorate.

In the run up to the election and shortly after results were out, the Voice of America set up a special service to broadcast a daily 30-minute radio programme in English during the week across Zimbabwe on medium wave. This had interviews with government and opposition politicians.

Supreme Court judgment on the state-owned media

The opposition Movement for Democratic Change took the ZBC, the Mass Media Trust, Zimbabwe Newspapers (see below) and the Minister of Information, Posts and Telecommunications to court to try and correct the bias of the state-owned media. Under the terms of a Provisional Order issued on 13 June the Supreme Court ruled that with immediate effect:

> *Zimbabwe Broadcasting Corporation and each and every person employed by it are required to perform its functions to carry on television and radio broadcasting services impartially, without discrimination on the basis of political opinion, and without hindering persons in their right to impart and receive ideas and information.*

The Supreme Court granted 15 working days to ZBC to show it why a Final Order confirming the Provisional Order should not be made. The Court's ruling also gave the Mass Media Trust and Zimbabwe Newspapers 15 days to show why a similar order should not be issued in respect to them. This term expired after the election.

The print media

The government-controlled Zimbabwe Newspapers was bought from the South African Argus Group shortly after independence in 1980. It is a listed company and publishes six papers. Although the company is quoted on the Zimbabwe Stock Exchange its shareholding is dominated by the government's Mass Media Trust, which owns 51 per cent. The editorial policy of Zimbabwe Newspapers is to support the government.

During the week, Zimbabwe Newspapers publishes two papers in English: the Harare-based *The Herald* is a daily with a circulation of 90,000 and the Bulawayo-based title, *The Chronicle*, also a daily, has a circulation of 40,000. Its weekly papers, published on Friday, are the English title, the *Manica Post* with a circulation of 19,000 and the Shona title, *Kwayedza*, with a circulation of 14,000.

In 1998, the privately-owned Associated Newspapers of Zimbabwe was started. Its flagship title is the *Daily News*, which is published Monday to Friday and has a circulation of 100,000. The other titles in this group are published on Friday. These are the Mutare-based *Eastern Star*, with a circulation of 15,000 and the Bulawayo-based *Despatch*, with a circulation of 20,000. ...

In contrast to the monopoly of the broadcast media, the newspapers in Zimbabwe publish a wide range of views. Senior staff at Zimbabwe Newspapers say that they tend to accentuate the positive sides of the government. They admit that in order to get a balanced picture of the news it is necessary to read the independent press. On the whole, the private press supported the opposition. ZANU PF rallies were covered prominently in *The Herald*, with attendance figures published being substantially higher than we saw.

During the period we were in Zimbabwe, the newspapers published robust editorials supporting either the governing party or the opposition. Many of the editorials in the government papers concentrated on government policy on land while those in the independent press reported that there was a desire for change in leadership and economic policy. Whilst both sectors of the print media reported incidents of campaign violence, reports of violence against opposition supporters tended to be carried by only the independent media.

During the election period, most print media did not attempt to educate voters until a few days before the polls. A notable exception to this was the *Financial Gazette*, which ten days before polling published a supplement titled 'Election 2000, Your Vote is Your Secret'. This carried policy statements of six different political parties in Shona, Ndebele and English, thereby widening the number of people who would read it. On the eve of voting, other papers carried similar supplements.

The Internet

This was used extensively by the opposition and its allies to spread their views within Zimbabwe and around the world. Some sites on the World Wide Web, which supported the opposition, were used as a repository of information for their sympathisers. Articles, particularly those from the international media which highlighted the difficulties faced by opposition supporters, were posted on these sites. Electronic mail was used by opposition allies to send information to their supporters and international observers. Many of these sites made no attempt to present balanced news.

The Media Monitoring Project

This was established in January 1999 and is a joint initiative of three organisations, the Zimbabwe Chapter of the Media Institute of Southern Africa (MISA), the Civic Education Network Trust (CENT) and Article 19, the international centre against censorship. The Media Monitoring Project Zimbabwe (MMPZ) is funded by the Norwegian International Development Agency (NORAD) and the Open Society Initiative for Southern Africa. It monitors the Zimbabwe media to determine how far they adhere to international and constitutionally guaranteed standards of freedom of expression, as well as generally accepted professional and ethical standards of journalism. The project has a particular interest in those sections of the media that are financed by public funds; however private media are also subject to scrutiny.

MMPZ issued weekly monitoring reports detailing the balance of coverage in the broadcast and print media. Ten days before the voting these became daily reports. These reports clearly indicate that ZBC and *The Herald* and other newspapers in the Zimbabwe papers stable were heavily biased in favour of the ruling party and the government. The opposition acknowledged this with a senior member of the MDC stating, 'We have written off the press for all practical purposes'.

Commonwealth Observer Group report

Sri Lanka Election, 2005

Note: *There were 13 candidates for the 2005 presidential election. Two emerged as the leading candidates – these were the incumbent Prime Minister Mahindra Rajapakse and opposition leader Ranil Wickremesinghe.*

Media

The [Commonwealth Observer Group] team noted that there are five companies spanning newspaper ownership, including eight Sinhalese, four Tamil and nine English language newspapers. There are five radio broadcasters and seven TV station owners.

One of the five large newspaper companies is a nationalised asset whose newspapers carry the bulk of government notifications and advertising. Significant sections of the private media are owned by relatives of key political figures in the country.

The team noted the highly partisan nature of media coverage of this Presidential election. The government-owned media appeared to show bias towards the candidacy of Mahindra Rajapakse, then Prime Minister, whilst the privately owned media showed a distinct bias towards the opposition leader, Ranil Wickremesinghe. These observations were supported by the domestic observer group PAFFREL.

During the time available to us, the team only monitored three daily English language newspapers and their sister publications on Sunday.

This perception of the media coverage appears to have persisted throughout the campaign and on polling day. Restrictions came into force at midnight on 14 November 2005 prohibiting public rallies and other forms of overt campaigning by the candidates.

Regulation of the media

The Commissioner of Elections has the power to appoint a competent authority in order to regulate the state media, if he considers it necessary. The team notes that the regulatory framework governing the scope, nature and timing of media coverage during political campaigns does not appear to be comprehensive.

2 Evolution of the Media's Role

Advent of Democracy

The media has reported on social and political events for centuries, yet its 'place at the dining table' in terms of elections coverage, especially in developing countries, is a fairly recent development. Such reporting has expanded in line with democracy and as gender and race-related barriers have diminished.

In many parts of Asia, Africa, the Caribbean and the Pacific, colonial rule ended only in the second half of the 20th century. In Africa, for example, Zimbabwe and Namibia achieved independence in 1980 and 1990, respectively, while Eritrea was born an independent state in 1991. Apartheid in South Africa ended with the country's first democratic elections in 1994.

For some countries in the former 'Eastern bloc' of what used to be communist Europe, democracy – and with it the concept of elections – arrived with the collapse of their centralised, socialist, single-party regimes from 1989. Boris Yeltsin was at the heart of the establishment of the Commonwealth of Independent States (CIS), the successor to the Union of Society Socialist Republics (USSR), only in December 1991.

Nor did the Americas have much of a head start. In the United States of America, it was not until 1965 that President Lyndon Johnson's signing into law of the Voting Rights Act ended voting discrimination against African-Americans. Latin America's democratic tradition was blighted by military dictatorship from the 1960s to the 1980s. Today, Cuba remains the only Latin American country under an unelected leader, with Raul Castro having replaced his brother Fidel, who overthrew Fulgencio Batista in 1959 in what is known as the Cuban revolution.

In his article, 'Formation of an Interstate System in East Asia', Ryuhei Hatsuse notes that the Philippines, South Korea, Taiwan and Thailand moved to genuine democracy in the late 1980s to the early 1990s. Indonesia achieved democracy in the late 1990s, but dictatorships still exist in North Korea, Vietnam and Myanmar.[13]

Scholar Eduardo Posada-Carbo (1996) argues that demo-

Generally, an independent media has evolved in tandem with the more general development of political freedoms.

cratic transitions in Latin America and Asia fuelled a growing interest in the study of democratisation and helped to foster increased optimism about the globalisation of democratic forms of government. At the centre of such study is the capacity of a country to regularly renew its contract with the people through periodic elections, electoral efficacy and the media's central role in enhancing democracy.

The 'Fourth Estate'

Critics of the popular school of pluralist liberal democracy see the media as fulfilling a vitally important role as guardians of democracy and defenders of the public interest. This school is premised upon the notion of the new-found power of 'the man of letters' (i.e. one devoted to scholarly or literary pursuits) and, by extension, the newspaper reporter. Proponents then argue that the mass media is 'the fourth estate',[14] adding to the three existing estates (as they were conceived in 19th century societies): the Priesthood, the Aristocracy and the Commons. Modern commentators attribute to the fourth estate a fourth power that checks and counterbalances the arms of government, namely the executive, legislature and the judiciary.

The media's role as a key player in the theatre of elections has evolved over time. Studies depict the evolution of the media in Europe, North America and Latin America with this notion of 'the fourth estate' offering a proactive check on the activities of governments, being increasingly incorporated into international law, although the practice has fallen somewhat short of the ideal.

Generally, an independent media has evolved in tandem with the more general development of political freedoms. Despite this evolution, there is a tendency for some sections of the media to reproduce the dominant (often conservative/bourgeois) culture and to represent the interests of those who own them. This tendency is attacked by (usually left-wing/liberal) critics. Others argue that the media has in reality moved away from the positive expectations of civil society, to become a vehicle of profiteering and propaganda for the politically powerful and social elite. Indeed, new studies show that globalisation and economic liberalisation have contributed to the media's having a negative and deteriorating attitude towards society. Thanks to global competition and the profit motive, the media has forgotten its social responsibility. These studies suggest that the media is no longer interested in contributing towards citizenship, providing a public sphere for dialogue and interaction among citizens. Instead, media institutions are busy transforming citizens into mere spectators, offering them entertainment instead of education, knowledge and information.

Broadcast Revolution

It should be noted that the concept of the 'fourth estate' referred only to print media, which for centuries – and certainly until 80 years ago – was the only journalistic form.

Print media had a limited reach, since functional literacy extended to a small proportion of the population only. The advent of broadcasting, therefore, was revolutionary in communicating social and political ideas to mass audiences to the extent that *The Danish Democracy Canon* argues that it expanded democracy exponentially.

Nonetheless, in many instances the very potential of radio and television was perceived to be a threat by political authorities, many of which were bent on controlling public debate. For example, the British Broadcasting Corporation (BBC) operated a '14-day rule' during the 1940s and 1950s, which prohibited coverage of any issue within two weeks of it being debated in the UK parliament. The compulsory blackouts of coverage of parties and candidates on the day before an election, which continue in countries like France, are also a relic of that period.

Times have changed. Modern elections in Western countries are dominated by television, a development that can be traced back to the first historic television debate between United States presidential candidates in 1960. The American model of television-mediated politics was initially resisted in many Western European countries, especially those with a long tradition of state-controlled broadcasting. The advent of commercial television in the 1980s helped to unshackle broadcasting regimes and usher in a new era of television politics.

For all the talk of 'spin doctors' and 'globalisation', much of what passes through the media at election times would be readily recognisable to a previous generation of voters, accustomed to a style of political campaigning through public meetings. The American tradition of paid television advertising, drawing upon the most sophisticated techniques of commercial advertising, is an important one, but it is not yet dominant worldwide. Europe's more regulated broadcasting still enjoys wide adherence during elections, more so than at any other time. A broadcaster in a regulated environment tends to favour lengthy policy messages and debate over quick sound bites.

Much as television has revolutionised elections reporting in the Western world, it is still only a growing feature of developing countries, where access is limited by poverty. People still grapple with basic facilities such as lack of electricity or water: owning a television set is the last thing on their minds. For these people, radio is their main source of election or any other news.

The Internet and Multimedia Communication

Innovation did not rest following the advent of radio and television. The next great transformation has taken place with the development of the Internet, which has radically changed the way in which elections are reported. It has effectively ended, for example, the practice of 'news blackouts' or 'reflection periods', since it operates largely beyond the reach of regulators.

More generally, the Internet has changed the way we work, play and communicate. It has led to a deliberate attempt by journalists to move from one form of communication – for example, either through print or broadcast – to multimedia forms. Ben Goldacre, contributor to UK newspaper *The Guardian*, tells of how he has moved from a primarily text medium to broadcast as well, and how he makes his work available online.[15]

The Internet is also changing the way presidential candidates wage campaigns and how voters make their voices heard.

Critical to this paradigm shift is the rapid growth of social networking – the Internet connecting people around the globe – which bears the potential to morph into a powerful tool for organising movements and setting political agendas. Journalist Jessica Guynn sees ample signs of this shift in the US presidential election in 2008:

> It is already clear that 2008 will be a watershed year in the evolution of the Internet, not only because it is now being used by massive amounts of online Americans to get political information, it is also being used extensively by mainstream media professionals in their efforts to cover the campaigns. So many of the stories in print, on TV and on the radio about the campaigns are origi-

nating online. In addition, 2008 is already shaping up to be the year where voter-generated content primarily through video will play an even bigger role in changing the dynamics of the campaign and continue to erode the candidates' attempt to control their message.[16]

Medium of the Future

In our view, the most significant innovation has been that of the mobile phone. Since their advent, only about 20 years ago, mobile phones have become easily accessible to rural and urban communities alike in the developing world, and in their wake access to telephones has leapfrogged an entire technological generation. Millions of people without access to a landline now own a mobile telephone, and text messages have already been used in political campaigning and in distributing campaign news.

TESTIMONY

Timothy Selemani – Kingdom of Swaziland

Every five years the nation's people converge in their 55 constituencies (*tinkhundla*) to cast votes and usher in a new government through the election of members of parliament. In Swaziland, electioneering begins at least a year before, with the process set in motion by the Chief Electoral Officer.

Elections were held in 2003 and the latest in September 2008, the latter being the first under a new constitution. However, both took place to elect independent candidates and were criticised by supporters of multi-party democracy, who prefer that candidates are voted for through political affiliation and not on an individual basis. Nevertheless, election fever in Swaziland has always had its fair share of interesting moments, events, joy, disputes and pain, as is the case in other African countries.

For purposes of this article, I will discuss only the August 2003 elections.

A year before the poll, prospective candidates for the election had started giving donations to members of their constituencies, secretly campaigning for the election. Legal procedure dictates that campaigning should commence only after a pronounce-ment by the Chief Electoral Officer, and it is illegal, according to the law, to buy votes by offering gifts and food to the electorate. However, politicians often find ways to circumvent the law. In my country, some politicians gave free soccer jerseys to soccer teams in front of television cameras, other paid school fees for orphaned and vulnerable children, whilst others just gave blankets, clothing and bread to the elderly.

It is worth noting is that the elderly (those over 60 years old) form about half the voting population. Very few among the youth participate in elections, and some of those interviewed said they had better things to do – a serious issue considering that the youth, as Commonwealth Secretary-General Kamalesh Sharma often says, are the ones who will inherit the 21st century.

About two months before the primary elections, the head of state has to dissolve parliament. Then the Chief Electoral Officer has to announce the dates for the nomination of new members, primary elections and secondary elections. No nominations are carried out at chiefs' residences (*imiphakatsi*), which are estimated to number more than 500 countrywide.

A few weeks before the 2003 elections, I went to Kontjingila to cover the nominations. A group of about 300 people sat under a tree and suggested names of people that could stand for the primary elections. Usually, about ten people get nominated for the primary elections, depending on the number of people that affiliate to the chief's residence. The group that showed up at Kontshingila predominantly comprised women and the elderly. Though few in number, those that raised their hands to nominate were men. The nominees were mostly men, too. The implication was that women were there to offer support and to show obedience to the authorities of the land. The process was long and the scorching heat resulted in the meeting loosing members. Immediately after the nominations, some of the nominees were congratulated by those still present.

> 'However, politicians often find ways to circumvent the law. In my country, some politicians gave free soccer jerseys to soccer teams in front of television cameras, other paid school fees for orphaned and vulnerable children, whilst others just gave blankets.'

One of the nominees was a head teacher who, just before the elections, offered gifts to people and even transported them to the chief's kraal in his car. The only woman nominee was the wife of the commissioner of Correctional Prisons. Although she campaigned strongly for the seat, many felt she had spent too many years living in the cities, far away from her constituency. Amongst the contenders, the head teacher won, whilst the commissioner's wife came second.

In the build-up to the primary and secondary elections, I went to Zombodze Emuva, another constituency in the southern part of Swaziland where campaigning was fierce. One of the favourites was a head teacher, although there was strong competition from a deputy sheriff. The Chief Electoral Officer facilitated the gathering of people in community halls, where the campaigning took place in the presence of election officers and the police. The teacher was a good public speaker, who managed to gain support from people, at times making outrageous promises such as building a hospital and an airport. The deputy sheriff specialised in giving donations such as blankets and money. His strategy did not work, however, as he lost the election to the teacher.

Then on the day of secondary election, I covered elections at Maseyisini, where a former cabinet minister was competing for a parliamentary seat with a former member of parliament (MP). There were many incidents of conflict involving the police and some voters, who had been declared frauds by electoral staff. It turned out the suspect illegal voters were a group of youth that were friends of the former minister's stepson. The former minister won the election, but it was later contested in court after the former MP said the election was rigged. The High Court of Swaziland ruled in favour of the MP, but said there should be new elections. The judgment raised serious concerns for some critics of the former minister, who said as a fraudulent voter, he should not be allowed near the polls again. In the by-election, the former minister won again, this time with a landslide victory.

Several other election results were contested in court, with bitter losers complaining, for example, that ballot papers were missing, some voters were illegal and so on. During the secondary election at Zombodze Emuva, the former head teacher also won, but was taken to court by his competitors who accused him of having used the name of the Queen Mother during his campaign. They said he had claimed to be favoured by the Queen Mother, and that he had brought in South Africans to vote for him. They further accused him of having cooked food for voters. The former head teacher won the court battle and was declared a substantive MP, after his opponents failed to produce evidence for their assertions.

After all 55 members of parliament had been voted in, they were sworn into parliament, where they were joined by 10 others appointed by His Majesty King Mswati III. From there, they elected their own speaker and deputy speaker to the House of Assembly. They also elected 10 members of the public to take Senate positions. The selection of MPs was rather unusual, as it comprised, among others, a musician and a journalist.

The Prime Minister was picked from the House of Assembly, as the Electoral Law states. He was appointed by the head of state. In turn, the prime minister appointed 16 cabinet ministers from the House of Assembly and the Senate. There was, however, a commotion in the House of Assembly when the elected speaker, Marwick Khumalo, was rejected by the national authorities for unstated reasons. A high-powered committee comprising traditional authorities was established to ensure that Khumalo vacated his seat. He grudgingly obliged.[17]

Commonwealth Observer Group report

Guyana Election, 2006

Note: *Ten political parties contested the 2006 national and regional elections. These were: the People's Progressive Party/Civic (PPP/C), which had as its presidential candidate Bharrat Jagdeo; the People's National Congress Reform-One Guyana (PNCR-1G), which fielded Robert Corbin as its presidential candidate; the Alliance for Change (AFC), which had Raphael Trotman; the Justice For All Party (JFAP), which had Chandra Narine Sharma; the Guyana Action Party/Rise, Organise and Rebuild (GAP/ROAR), which had Paul Hardy as its presidential candidate; and The United Force (TUF), which fielded Manzoor Nadir. These six parties contested the geographic constituencies, which qualified them for the national elections and thus their entitlement to field a presidential candidate. The other four parties only contested regional elections.*

Media role

... The news media played a significant role in fostering the atmosphere for a peaceful campaign, notwithstanding some breaches of the media code of conduct. Noticeably reduced from the airwaves was the diet of wild rumours, inflammatory statements and accusations, which served only to fuel flames of fear, doubt, tensions and confusion during election campaigns in the past.

We shared the concerns expressed by the Commonwealth Observer Group of the 2001 Elections about the damage that could be done to the democratic process through free-wheeling news and information media and therefore welcomed the establishment of the Media Monitoring Unit and the Independent Media Refereeing Panel.

Guyana has one radio station owned and controlled by the government. However, there are a number of independently owned television stations with less coverage than the government-run radio and television station.

State media

It was drawn to our attention that National Communications Network (NCN)-TV gave the incumbent party (PPP/C) an unfair advantage in the elections. Examples included: the repeated replaying of President Jagdeo's congratulations to the Guyana team that won the Stanford 20/20 cricket tournament; the replaying of a documentary-type presentation on the President's contacts with world leaders, combined with references to his plans for Guyana's future development; and the replay of 'interviews with presidential candidates', which repeated the interview with President Jagdeo.

Voter education

The general consensus was that the media could have played a better role in getting voter education to the public on time. However, due to the short time available between the announcement of the election date and the elections themselves, there was little time to inform the electorate of where they would be voting, particularly because there had been an increase in polling stations.

Election advertisements

The inequitable distribution of advertisements was questioned by *Stabroek News*, which stated that the elections were a national issue and therefore placements of public notices in the newspapers should be unbiased as was the case during the elections. Our observation was that the *Guyana Chronicle* carried most of the public notices and advertisements to the exclusion of the *Stabroek* and *Kaieteur* newspapers ...

Code of conduct and media monitoring

Guyana's media organisations signed a code of conduct for the media, which committed them to provide fair, balanced and accurate information, including voter education, to help deliver successful elections by enabling voters to make informed decisions at the ballot box. The code of conduct also outlined the role of the media organisations to provide minimum equal shares of free airtime/newspaper space in the period after Nomination Day in the lead-up to Election Day. The recommended amount would be at least five minutes of airtime a week for radio and television, and a minimum of 200 words per week for print.

> **The code of conduct also outlined the role of the media organisations to provide minimum equal shares of free airtime/newspaper space in the period after Nomination Day in the lead-up to Election Day. The recommended amount would be at least five minutes of airtime a week for radio and television, and a minimum of 200 words per week for print.**

An Independent Media Monitoring and Refereeing Panel (IMMRP), comprising veteran journalists Lennox Grant of Trinidad and Tobago and Wyvolyn Gager of Jamaica, was established to monitor the media's adherence to the code of conduct. This Panel was chosen by local journalists.

Overview

The Media Monitoring Unit (MMU) set up by GECOM [Guyana Elections Commission] produced a series of reports on the conduct of the Guyanese media. In a survey conducted between 25 July and 5 August, during the period after Nomination Day, the MMU concluded that the state-owned National Communication Network (NCN) Channel 11, which has a major share of viewership (about 80 per cent of the population), had not achieved the level of balance envisaged in the Media Code of Conduct. The MMU said it noticed that television hosts and reporters of Government Information Agency (GINA) presented their opinions rather than facts in their programmes. NCN's Voice of Guyana radio network, which broadcast on AM 560, reflected a similar imbalance in its election coverage. The MMU noted that the proportion of positive coverage outside of news between the two main parties was 3:1 in favour of the ruling party.

Election coverage on other television stations ranged from well balanced to one-sidedness, with a few in between. GWTV Channel 2 favoured the PNCR-1G, but they gave the PPP/C ruling party a substantial on-air profile, followed by AFC and TUF. CNS Channel 6, owned by JFAP leader CN Sharma, gave extensive coverage to his political party with some coverage of PPP/C and other parties in the lead-up to the elections. But this changed positively closer to the elections …

This trend of election coverage by the various television stations continued in the two weeks leading up to polling day, though the MMU also reported the use of inflammatory and libellous remarks on some of the partisan television stations, which was in breach of the Media Code of Conduct and journalistic principles of fair, accurate, balanced and responsible reporting.

Radio

The state-owned National Communications Network (NCN) operates two radio stations – Voice of Guyana at AM 560 and the music channel Hot FM 98.1. The Presidential Secretariat expressed its concern over the establishment of an illegal radio transmission on FM 98.3 weeks before the polls. The broadcasts included PNCR-1G political advertisements and allegedly antisocial exhortations to Guyanese in between its music programmes. The government tried to identify the location of the illegal transmission, which was believed to be in the Linden area. The establishment of this pirate radio station using a frequency close to NCN's Hot FM 98.1 was aimed at providing an avenue for a different political voice – that of the opposition.

Print media

The MMU stated that the three English language daily newspapers – the *Guyana Chronicle*, *Kaieteur News* and *Stabroek News* – provided reasonable coverage of the political parties. It was noted that the state-owned *Guyana Chronicle* provided coverage for all six parties. The *Guyana Chronicle* was seen to give less negative coverage to PNCR-1G than either *Stabroek News* or *Kaieteur News*, while *Kaieteur News* gave more positive coverage to AFC than *Stabroek News*. Overall *Stabroek News* gave more than two-thirds of its coverage to PPP/C compared to the *Guyana Chronicle*.

Political party advertisements

There was controversy over some political advertisements. One PPP/C advertisement, which disparaged the PNCR-1G through the use of inflammatory language, was repeatedly aired on NCN and several other television channels. It showed scenes of people from a particular ethnic group attacking buildings during previous periods of unrest in the country. With the song 'The Great Pretender' playing in the background, the voice-over said: 'Everyone in Guyana remembers well the role PNC/AFC leaders played out on the streets of the city. Yet today they want you to believe they've changed their ways and can lead Guyana. Can you believe the promises of the PNC/AFC?'

The advertisement linked the leaders of PNCR-1G, Robert Corbin, and AFC, Raphael Trotman, to the rioting and looting through the use of images and accusatory words. A more judicious editorial judgement on the content of political party advertisements in line with the Media Code of Conduct should have been made by the television stations concerned to be mindful of the impact of this politically charged and provocative advertisement that could instil fear and suspicion, exacerbate racial tensions, and even incite unrest and violence.

Two television stations – VCT Channel 28, which was owned by a PNCR-1G candidate, and WRHM Channel 7 – declined to air the advertisement, citing concerns over its contents. The PPP/C accused the two stations of attempting to 'muzzle the PPP/C's message to the Guyanese electorate' and said it would air the advertisement with increased frequency on other television stations. The IMMRP said the Media Code of Conduct upheld the right of media organisations to make judgements in favour of good taste and respect for public safety and decency. They said the media organisations could refuse material likely to be hateful, ethnically offensive, or likely to promote public disorder or threaten the security of the state.

There was also a PPP/C complaint about a PNCR-1G television advertisement, involving a letter purportedly written by an Amerindian child, which triggered a response from the PNCR-1G leader about his party's inclusiveness. However, the leader went on to say that he also had Amerindian blood. This was seen as an appeal to race, which could be offensive to other ethnic groups of Guyana. It was therefore a violation of the spirit and intent of the Media Code of Conduct, the Media Refereeing Panel ruled.

Electronic communications

The political parties did not capitalise on the Internet to spread their message locally and abroad, particularly to aid their efforts to reach out to the Guyanese diaspora for both political and financial support. Not all the parties contending the elections had set up a website. For the parties that did, it was noticed that some of these websites were not regularly updated. The websites of the PPP/C at *www.voteppc.com*, PNCR-1G's *www.guyanapnc.org* and AFC's *www.afcguyana.com* were most informative on their political leaders and electoral candidates and their agenda, besides featuring speeches, press releases and news about their rallies.

The PPP/C website provided comprehensive information on its activities, including the presidential candidate's speeches, a photo gallery of the party leader's activities, press releases and information on press conferences and videos of the press conferences. The website also posted the GECOM election results. The PNCR-1G posted information on its Central Executive Committee members on its website, and also sought new membership among web visitors. It also had a very accessible email address for correspondence.

AFC's website featured its party constitution, election candidates, besides audio-visuals, a photo gallery of its activities and election posters. The website also listed its political rallies and opinion polls conducted by the party. It also encouraged membership and donations to the AFC. The United Force's website www.tufsite.com provided basic information on the party, its manifesto (however the hyperlink was broken, which did not allow web visitors to view the manifesto) and election candidates. The news articles were not up to date. The GAP-ROAR's website *www.gap-roar.org* posted some basic information on its political candidates and plans.

A novel feature of the campaign was telephone canvassing. Many cell phone subscribers reported receiving messages from at least four of the contesting parties. The AFC announced that part of its strategy was for an army of 500 to 600 supporters in North America to call up electors and requests their votes.

Opinion polls

Several opinion polls were conducted in the lead-up to polling day. Results varied. For example, opinion polls conducted by the North American Teachers Association (NACTA) showed the PPP/C and AFC making gains among the electorate, with the PNCR-1G losing ground. A poll conducted on 20 August predicted that the PPP/C could garner between 43 per cent and 51 per cent support, but would still be short of an overall majority of parliamentary seats. NACTA projected a loss of seats for PPP/C and PNCR-1G at this year's elections, with the beneficiaries being the AFC and JFAP. The findings were based on a survey involving more than a thousand voters.

An opinion poll conducted by the AFC through Arcop, a Mexico-based pollster, on 16 August posited encouraging gains in popularity for the AFC, rising in percentage points from 24 per cent on 8 August to 27 per cent on 16 August. The other political parties were shown to have dropped in popularity, except for PPP/C which was listed as gaining 6 percentage points on 16 August from the previous week.

Commonwealth Observer Group report

Kenya Election, 2007

Note: *Kenya's controversial 2007 election was an electoral battle that pitted a coalition led by incumbent President Mwai Kibaki against an umbrella opposition group under the banner the Orange Democratic Movement, led by Raila Odinga.*

Media

... During the 2007 elections in Kenya, various media outlets – print, radio and electronic – generally played a positive role in disseminating information on the electoral process to the voting population of Kenya ...

... Our overall impression was that the majority of the media did an excellent job in informing the voting public on the political issues relevant to the election. It was difficult to discern any overt bias, which had been a concern expressed by a number of commentators.

However, we noted that the public-owned media, Kenya Broadcasting Corporation (KBC), which is required by law to provide equal and balanced coverage to all political parties participating in the elections, was biased in favour of the Party for National Unity (PNU), as the party in government. This observation was confirmed by media monitoring that was carried out during the electoral period. This is regrettable.

The Kenya Broadcasting Corporation Act (the Act) was amended in 1997 to regulate KBC's coverage of political activities during elections. The Act provides for equal coverage of campaign activities for all political parties and their presidential candidates. It was quite clear that KBC failed to comply with this legislative requirement.

The Act also required that KBC, in consultation with the ECK [Electoral Commission of Kenya], allocate free broadcasting to registered political parties participating in the election, but this was not done. The Chairman of the ECK publicly complained that KBC had refused to comply. It appeared there was little effective action the ECK could take. We are of the view that there is a need to implement better methods of obtaining compliance with these two legislative requirements during the election campaign. Considerable media coverage was given to decisions taken by the government right up to the eve of the election. This can give an unfair advantage to an incumbent government. Elsewhere in this report we suggest a moratorium on major decision making in the lead up to an election.

The media, particularly the print media, paid particular attention to the role of the Electoral Commission of Kenya, and the whole electoral regime. Most aspects of the electoral process were extensively covered and reported on. There were also some very insightful analyses and commentaries authored and published in the major newspapers, namely, *The Nation* and *The Standard*. Furthermore, most television stations ran special election-related programmes to inform voters about their rights and well as providing a platform for the major candidates to espouse their programmes and manifestos.

In the lead up to the elections, the Media Council of Kenya, ECK and media practitioners developed guidelines aimed at ensuring responsible media coverage, upholding journalistic professional standards, impartiality and independence. These were often flouted. It is not clear how they were enforced and how errant media were sanctioned. Observers were told that the media in Kenya have political leanings that are influenced by ownership, ethnic considerations, and business interests. We were, however, not able to independently verify these accusations. The media gave full coverage of incidences of election-related violence, and in some cases carried articles condemning the violence and calling for peaceful and fair elections.

Sectarian ethnic campaigning by some politicians was denounced in media editorials. However, there were some stories which reported on allegations where it was clear that there was no evidence to substantiate the reports. Such stories, which put unjustified doubt in the voters' minds, are to be deplored. In some cases, the stories led to outbreaks of violence. There is a need to impose better discipline on media that undertake such reporting. Journalists and the media must conduct their duties responsibly by seeking and reporting facts. They should desist from reporting rumour and inflammatory statements that lack authenticity.

There were also instances of anonymous advertisements being published that encouraged voters to support certain political parties. There appeared to be no restriction on the amount of money that could be spent on political advertising, furthermore there appeared to be no consistency with regard to the standards required for election advertising, particularly with regard to the ability of the media to decline advertising on the grounds of taste and decency. We recommend that consideration is given to require all advertisements to carry some form of identification as well as clearer guidelines with regard to disallowing advertising.

3 The Media and the Electoral Process

After tracking developments in the history of the media, we now turn to its role in the electoral process. The media takes part in the various stages of the electoral process, starting before the campaign period and ending with post-voting reports.

The Danish Democracy Canon outlines the basis for the media's involvement. It argues that representative democracy rests on certain preconditions: that the population actively keeps abreast of societal developments; that the various groups become clear in their own mind about how they can benefit their own interests and at the same time contribute to creating a better society; and that each group finds the best-suited person to promote and defend their interests. None of these goals can be achieved in the absence of a free and vibrant media.

The extent to which the media plays a significant role in an election is determined by the degree of media development and diversification in any individual setting. Each country has its own circumstances and media environment, which means that citizens around the globe have different levels and forms of access to the media.

In Western Europe, the Internet and other technological advances have modified a media landscape dominated by television. In countries where access to television is limited, aural communication (usually radio) is the dominant media form. In addition, traditions of respect for free expression and other media rights determine the qualitative characteristics of elections and democracy.

Whatever their circumstances, citizens in any democracy are united by three rights:

- The right of voters to make a fully informed choice

- The right of candidates to put their policies across

- The right of the media to report and express its views on matters of public interest

As has been referred to above, these rights are encapsulated in the freedom of expression guaranteed in Article 19 of the Universal Declaration of Human Rights. They should apply at all times, and not just in the run-up to or during elections. In particular, the media should look out for how far media freedom and pluralism are respected during an election period, because this is a good indication of general respect for freedom of expression in a country, itself an essential precondition for a functioning democracy. In addition, an election can be an ideal opportunity to educate government on its obligation to respect and nurture media freedom, and to educate the media itself on its responsibilities in the democratic process.

The media ought to be present and active from the pre-campaign period to the installation of the new government and elected officials. The audit of a government's first 100 days in office has also become a standard engagement for media players. This period usually provides the first glimpses of whether a government will meet its election pledges or whether it will be derailed by other concerns or priorities.

Similarly, media activity is often regulated by specific requirements set out in national electoral laws. Such regulations include the duration of campaigns, the existence of a campaign period or a period of silence or reflection, and the rights of parties and candidates. These regulations differ across countries, but agree on the universal principle that the media is present to report, inform and educate.

In its handbook for election observers, the European Commission lists seven examples of best practice that the media should adhere to during an election. These are that:

- Regulatory authorities ensure the media's coverage of elections meets legal requirements

- All broadcast media provide balanced and impartial coverage of the election, as well as non-discriminatory and equitable levels of access for contestants

- State-owned or publicly owned media provide free print space to the candidates or parties in a non-discriminatory and equitable manner

- The conditions for contestants to purchase paid for political advertising are non-discriminatory, with standardised rates for all contestants

- The media airs debates among candidates following clear and mutually agreed rules and procedures

- The media co-operates with the Election Management Board (or electoral commission) in voter education

- The media portrays women, as well as men, as serious candidates and political leaders[18]

Media participation takes place in a variety of ways and does not follow a specific script. Some media programmes provide direct communication between the political community and citizens. Others provide analysis, debates and interviews with candidates, while others report and comment on the candidates' activities. Politicians often seek access to certain types of media content not directly linked to campaigns, because such content attracts large audiences. In the United States election in 2008, for example, Republican Party candidate Senator John McCain and his running mate Sarah Palin both appeared on the popular NBC satirical show 'Saturday Night Live' at a time when their campaign was flagging, winning free visibility and showcasing their funnier, human side on a programme with an audience of millions of people. All media content that is political in nature requires monitoring and evaluation for fairness and balance.

Pre-campaign Issues

The notion of pre-campaign issues presupposes that there is a specified campaign period. While this is the case in many developing countries, some nations, such as the United States, effectively impose no limits on the time allowed for campaigning. In many systems, there may be little time between presidential, legislative, local or provincial elections. However, under any electoral system, there are issues relating to media coverage that occur, essentially, outside election periods. These are voter education (a principle area) and discussion of the electoral system.

Civic education

According to the *Stanford Encyclopaedia of Philosophy*, civic education, whenever and however undertaken, prepares the people of a country, especially the young, to carry out their role as citizens. Civic education is, therefore, political education or, as Amy Gutmann describes it, 'the cultivation of the virtues, knowledge and skills necessary for political participation' (1987, p. 287). Of course, in some regimes, political participation and therefore civic education may be limited or even negligible.[19]

The media should report on civic education, which is an essential aspect in ensuring that citizens know their roles, responsibilities and obligations.

Voter education

Voter education specifically relates to dissemination of information on the government and its democratic credentials, as well as on the various agendas the other competing parties stand for.

Some countries, such as Kenya, include voter education in an elections guide provided by their electoral commission, while others, like Thailand, have this issue reinforced in the country's constitution. For example, Thailand's constitution exhorts the 1998 Electoral Commission to 'provide or co-ordinate with any state agency, local government, state enterprise, or to support a private organisation, to provide education to the people on the democratic regime of government with the King as Head of the State'.[20] The country's Electoral Commission takes this mandate seriously and its Public Participation Bureau comprises departments dedicated to non-governmental organisations and voter activist groups, provincial public participation, election campaigns, media and information dissemination.

There is a clear connection between civic/voter education and the electoral system in media coverage. Informed debate about the electoral system can only take place in the context of thorough public education on how that system actually works. At the same time, pre-campaign voter education is likely to focus on a number of issues, depending on the electoral system and the political context. Such issues include who is eligible to vote, why it is important to be on the voters' roll and how to register to vote, and the splitting of electoral areas into constituencies.

Another important issue is what systems exist in order to ensure fair coverage and access by political parties outside election campaign periods. Many countries have systems that allow political parties regular opportunities to put across their views to the electorate in direct-access programmes. Similar systems are used to allocate direct-access slots during elections. These are issues of concern to legislators and broadcasting regulators more than they are to election administrators. Nonetheless, such issues have an important bearing on maintaining a level playing field in election coverage.

A further fundamental issue for legislators and broadcasting regulators is the independence of publicly funded media from the government and ruling parties. The opportunity for direct access during an election campaign is helpful up to a point only. If the general tenor of broadcasting outside campaign periods is strongly biased, then it is difficult to establish a level playing field during election periods.

Campaign Issues

For most media in the developing world, the start of the campaign period is when election coverage really takes off. This is the time when the media will seek accreditation by the electoral commission or management board to secure unfettered access. Smooth running of the regulatory process depends largely on systems put in place before an election. By this stage, a number of fundamental questions should already have been answered, with the media and political parties having a clear understanding of their roles and responsibilities. These questions include:

- What laws or regulations govern media coverage of the campaign?

- Who is responsible for implementing these laws and regulations?

- How is direct-access broadcasting regulated?

- What regulations govern paid political advertising?

- What policies are there on bigoted speech (i.e. speech intended to degrade, intimidate or incite violence or prejudicial action)?

- What policies are there on defamation?

- What policies or miscellaneous provisions are there on issues such as news blackouts or opinion polls?

- What mechanisms are in place for aggrieved individuals or organisations to lodge complaints?

It is absolutely essential that these issues should be agreed upon in advance of the campaign. Determining such important policy questions on an ad hoc basis will diminish the authority of the supervisory body and create the impression that some sections of

In a well-managed election, the supervisory body must ensure maximum flow of information to the media.

the media are receiving preferential treatment. Ideally, the media-related functions of a supervisory or regulatory body during the campaign period are: first, to monitor adherence to agreed international standards, rules and regulations, and procedures, and to take whatever action is necessary to secure this; and second, to provide the media with all the necessary information to report the electoral process effectively and accurately.

Keeping the media informed

In a well-managed election, the supervisory body must ensure maximum flow of information to the media. There are basically two reasons for this. First, assuming that informing the media is the same as informing the public, then a constant flow of information enables the electorate to exercise its democratic rights and retain its confidence in the election process. Second, assuming that the media will cover the election regardless of the actions of the supervisory body, then it is in everyone's interest that the media content is as accurate as possible.

Consequently, in addition to its role of media regulation, the electoral supervisory body must also devote resources to information management. There are three fundamental principles of such management in an election situation. First, the election administration must make available the maximum amount of information, barring only that information whose disclosure would compromise the integrity of the election process. Second, all information released by the election administration must be accurate to the best of its knowledge. Third, information must be released on a non-discriminatory basis to all media, regardless of their ownership or political affiliation.

These principles are significant in that if they are breached, the objectives of informing the electorate and maintaining its confidence in the process will be damaged, sometimes irreparably.[21] In countries with a history of censorship or control over the flow of information, these three principles may represent a break with old habits. However, the temptation to hold back information or to provide it selectively to favoured journalists is one that electoral officials must resist.

A practical problem in both new and old democracies is to ensure the consistency of information emanating from the electoral supervisory body. The appointment of a press officer or creation of a media department should ensure that the authority speaks with a single voice and that the media knows where to find information. Some common techniques to keep the media informed include training of journalists, issuing press releases, media briefings (or press conferences), providing briefing packs and establishing a media centre (i.e. a central location that serves as a one-stop for media on any official information related to the electoral process). A sample press release is shown below.

Box 3.1 Sample press release

ELECTORAL COMMISSION OF ZAMBIA
Ndeke Annex, Haile Sellasie Avenue, PO Box 50274, LUSAKA

13 April 2006

PRESS RELEASE
(*For Immediate Release*)

INSPECTION OF PROVISIONAL VOTERS' ROLL TO BE ANNOUNCED SOON

The Electoral Commission of Zambia will soon announce the dates within which the Provisional Voters' Roll shall be displayed for inspection. All those who registered during the registration of voters exercise will be required to go to the Registration Centres where they registered with their Green National Registration Cards to inspect and verify that their particulars in the register are correct.

Details to look out for:

- Correct photograph
- Correct name
- Correct date of birth
- Correct NRC number
- Correct voters' card number
- Correct address

Remember, the inspection period is 14 days ONLY.

Signed

Jeremy Titus Obulinji
MEDIA ADVISER, ELECTORAL COMMISSION OF ZAMBIA.
Contact: jtobulinji@eck.org.zm and +260 977 444 444

Voter information

An important function of the media during campaign periods is to be a constant provider of voter information. This includes formal voter educational material, which by definition is non-partisan, and content from election coverage, which may contain highly partisan material. Voter education through the mass media may be expensive and may consequently assume a low priority in environments where cost is a major consideration. However, on occasion the media themselves may undertake to produce their own voter education material or to offer their services 'at cost' to the electoral authorities. This type of initiative would usually be expected of private media in a country where public media is strongly controlled by the government and where the political opposition is given no airtime or hearing by state-owned media.

The scope of voter information material can extend beyond traditional methods of communication – from advertisements telling people how to vote to educational soap operas. Voter education must be targeted at traditionally disadvantaged communities, who are generally less likely to register to vote or participate in elections. Such communities include women, racial, ethnic or national minorities, and people with disabilities. With special programming – which is tailored to reach a specific constituency and which falls out of a broadcaster's usual retinue of news bulletins and features, for example, the use of minority languages – the mass media (and especially broadcasters) can play a critical role in promoting popular participation.

However, voter information is much broader than voter education, and this is the rationale behind electoral administrators investing time and resources in keeping the mass media adequately briefed on developments. At the same time, the media should be proactive in scrutinising election arrangements and exposing any shortcomings. This is an important aspect of the transparency and accountability of an election process.

Promoting professional media coverage

The responsibility for promoting professional media coverage of elections lies primarily with the media organisations themselves. The role of the electoral administration is to create an environment in which such professionalism can take place. However, there are also numerous elements of editorial coverage in which there may be specific regulations regarding what the media may or may not say, hence the direct involvement of a regulatory body. Such elements include:

- ## *Coverage of opinion polls*

  Many countries have explicit regulations governing how opinion polls may be reported. In some cases, for example in France, reporting of opinion poll findings is prohibited on the day before and the actual day of the election. However, total prohibition of opinion poll reporting is no longer a practical proposition. The argument in favour of some form of regulation in this respect is that the public may not be aware of the limitations of opinion polling and may be unduly influenced by their findings. On the other hand, developing professional coverage in this area is probably best achieved by disseminating guidelines on how to report opinion polls, rather than by prohibiting their misreporting.

- ## *Special information programming*

  The one element of media coverage where regulation is usually considered necessary is 'special programming', which usually consists of candidate debates and panel interviews. Some countries with a long history in this area have developed standard formats without any external regulation. Others, especially newer democracies, have developed detailed rules to ensure that all participants in the debate have fair access. The Independent Elections Commission of South Africa is a good example of this.

- ## *Government activities and campaigning*

  One way in which media coverage is commonly abused is by manipulation of government functions for campaign purposes. For instance, senior officials running for re-election may dubiously place themselves in the public eye in carrying out their official functions. This happens in almost all countries and is to a large extent a matter that should be left to the good professional judgement of the media itself. However, it may be necessary to establish guidelines to prevent abuse, especially where the public media is accustomed to heavy reporting of government officials' functions. During presidential by-elections in Zambia in October 2008 to fill the post made vacant by President Levy Mwanawasa's death, opposition leader Michael Sata accused Acting President Rupiah Banda of abusing the power and influence provided by incumbency by using state infrastructure to campaign. In the event, Banda won the election by a razor-thin margin.

- *News blackouts/'reflection periods'*

  Countries like France and Italy operate a statutory or voluntary blackout period on election news at some point during the campaign.[22] This often takes place once voting has started, to avoid misleading and abusive last-minute campaigning. Sometimes blackouts can extend for several days before the election, to create a 'reflection period' during which voters digest information received during the campaigns. Some countries have found it necessary to impose news bans on security grounds. In Kenya, where 'blackouts' or 'reflection periods' do not exist, the government imposed a news blackout in the aftermath of the disputed December 2007 elections, arguing that the media was inciting hatred and violence. This led to a sharp rebuke from media NGOs such as Reporters Without Borders (see text box, below). Global organisations such as the Commonwealth Secretariat also called for a reversal of the ban, which was eventually lifted on 5 February 2008.

Box 3.2 Government imposes 'dangerous and counterproductive' news blackout

Warning the government of the dangers of the ban on live radio and TV news reports that it announced yesterday, Reporters Without Borders today condemned the climate of fear imposed on the privately owned media in the wake of Kenya's disputed presidential election.

Source: *http://www.rsf.org/article.php3?id_article=24913* [accessed 8 January 2009]

Special information programming

The most common form of 'special information programming' during election campaigns is the candidates' debate. A variant of this is the panel interview. These special formats are unusual in that they fall somewhere between regular editorial programming and direct-access slots. In some countries, the only form of direct access available is an interview or debate. This unusual and hybrid type of programming means that a special set of rules has emerged in most places where they are conducted. These rules are established by law, self-regulation and by custom and practice.

For example, although the rules governing US Television debates have evolved by convention, broadcasters must still abide by the equal opportunities rule under the Federal Communications Act. The rule stipulates, among other things, that while a broadcaster may choose which candidates to invite to take part in a debate, the chosen candidates must then be afforded equal opportunities. This rule effectively allows broadcasters to exclude minor candidates from debates, leaving Democrat and Republican candidates only. In the recent past, some minor candidates have threatened to take legal action after their exclusion from televised debates.

Certainly in Africa, not everyone agrees that candidate debates are a good thing. In 1992, the then-ruling Kenya African National Union (KANU) party argued that debates could create artificial discord, even promoting ethnic hatred. It may be claimed that political discourse becomes too personalised, as head-to-head debates underline the 'horse-race' nature of political campaigning, providing all style and no substance. In Zimbabwe (2001, 2005 and 2008), Mozambique (2004) and Zambia (2001 and 2006), challengers sought to hold presidential debates while incumbents did not favour debates and bluntly refused to participate.

TV debate proponents disagree, contending that none of these arguments is overwhelming. They say it is unacceptable to demonise vigorous discussion, just because these may have spilt into violence in the past. In any case, they argue, a 20-second advertisement could do more to degrade the quality of political discourse than a lengthy live debate.

There is little disagreement that live TV debates are particularly suited to presidential campaigning. Broader campaigns for national and local elections do not lend themselves to this campaign format, although there will often be other forms of special programming in which leading candidates may be questioned on their policies.

Candidates are often interviewed in formalised settings. Sometimes, as Zimbabwe's 2000 elections showed, special format interviews may be almost the only opportunity that parties have to speak directly to the electorate on their policies. In these circumstances, it is advisable to have an agreed format, although this would not normally be governed by rules and regulations. The aim for participating parties would be to have a balance of political allegiances among the journalists conducting the interviews, as well as a balance of issues, not reflecting the agenda of any one party.

At other times, broadcasters may have phone-in discussions in which the electorate can address questions directly to politicians. Such programmes can suffer the deficiencies of all phone-ins, namely rambling, self-important and ill-informed callers (not unlike some politicians, we might add). However, they can also offer sensationally effective examination of policies.

Allocation of time to candidates and parties

Almost invariably, the public media is thought to have a duty to publish or broadcast election statements by competing parties. It is also generally accepted that the publicly funded media is obligated to allow parties and their candidates to communicate directly with the electorate. Beyond that, however, there are many issues to be determined.

The main question is whether direct access by political parties should be free or paid, or a mixture of the two. Different rules are often adopted for print and broadcast media. Sometimes all parties are allocated free direct access, but can top this up with paid advertising. The second question concerns the division of time or space among the parties. In a system of paid advertising this may not be an issue, as time is simply allocated to those who can pay.[23] In other circumstances, how can a regulatory body allocate direct-access broadcasts to political parties? What criteria need to be taken into account to split the available time: equality (every party gets equal time); equitability or fairness (parties are allocated time according to perceived or alleged popular support); past electoral support (the number of seats currently held in parliament or the percentage of the popular vote received in previous elections); on the basis of opinion polls conducted by reputable non-partisan organisations; or according to the number of candidates running?

The third issue is timing of slots. Some related questions include:

- Will there be regulation on the times that the slots are broadcast?

- If all concerned were to get a chance to broadcast during prime time, how should the slots be allocated?

- In what order should the parties be allowed to broadcast?

Who pays and who makes the programmes is the fourth issue. For example, will parties be responsible for making their own broadcasts or will the public broadcaster facilitate such productions? In either case, who foots the bill?

The final issue is who decides what gets broadcasted. Related questions include:

- Does the regulatory body have any say in the content of direct-access broadcasts or political advertising?

- Can the parties basically say what they like?

- If not, what are their limits?

Dealing with paid political advertising

The decision to allow paid political advertising on radio or TV depends heavily on the structure and conduct of a country's broadcasting industry and the type of regulatory system in place. It is curious that the issue of paid political advertising in newspapers is scarcely controversial. The universal practice is that advertising is permitted, subject only to limitations such as campaign spending ceilings and restrictions on content (although the state media does not always accept this aspect).

The fact that many countries have different rules for political advertising on radio and television is attributable to advertising costs being higher in broadcasting than in print media. It may also be due to broadcasters being either publicly owned or receiving part of their frequency spectrum from a public body. Of course, neither of these explanations automatically leads to a prohibition of political advertising over the airwaves. However, they do explain the different approaches to print and broadcast media.

Broadly speaking, countries with a long tradition of public broadcasting – for example, Britain, Denmark and France – tend to be hostile to paid political advertising. Those with a stronger commercial broadcasting tradition, such as the United States, tend to regard political advertising as natural. It is notable that Finland – the European country with the highest levels of commercial broadcasting – should also be the one where unrestricted political advertising is permitted. This is the general tendency, but there are many exceptions. Canada, for example, which has a public broadcasting tradition similar to Britain's, has an approach to political advertising that is much closer to that of the United States. Neither is the issue necessarily to do with whether a public broadcaster accepts commercial advertising: the BBC has always prohibited commercial advertising, but French public broadcasting has permitted it since the 1960s; yet each maintains a strict embargo on political advertising. A common pattern is for public broadcasters to provide free direct-access slots according to predetermined criteria, while private broadcasters sell advertising slots to parties and candidates, often on different criteria. This is the case in Germany and in Italy.

Government activities and campaigning

Incumbents will usually try to use their official position to their own advantage. A president running for re-election may schedule important meetings to bolster his or her image as a statesman or woman. This is an inevitable, if slightly unsavoury, aspect of democratic campaigning. However, there are limits. If a government minister used his or her official telephone to mobilise for his or her party or vehicles to carry voters, such action would be denounced as an abuse of public funds. Most developing countries have guidelines on the use of official vehicles during an election. In India, all cars carrying officials have to be registered with the Electoral Commission as part of its attempts to cut abuse.[24]

Often the reprimand in such cases should be directed against the officials concerned rather than the media. Yet journalists still need to be educated to judge the real news value of Minister X opening a new pig farm (or whatever). In the case of the state-owned media, a firmer hand may be needed not to censor or interfere in editorial freedom, but to ensure the proper use of public funds. Programmes featuring government officials using their regular official engagements as part of a campaign to be re-elected should be strictly avoided.

In Malawi's 1999 elections, the High Court made an important ruling relating to broadcast coverage of presidential functions (see text box). It found that while this was a perfectly normal and proper role of the public broadcaster, the broadcaster was duty bound to give equivalent opportunity to the opposition if campaign messages were included in such broadcasts. Similar regulations may also apply to direct-access material. This ruling could provide key lessons elsewhere.

Box 3.3 Favouring ruling party violates Constitution, rules court

THE HIGH COURT of Malawi, Mkandawire J presiding, ordered the Malawi Broadcasting Corporation (MBC) to give equitable coverage to all political parties and all presidential candidates in the general election held last May. It held that the live coverage by MBC (Malawi Broadcasting Corporation) of the incumbent president's rallies during which campaign statements promoting the ruling party were made not only violated the Communications Act and the Parliamentary and Presidential Elections Act, but also amounted to unfair discrimination, which was contrary to section 20 of the Malawi Constitution.

Source: Article 19 – *http://www.fxi.org.za/pages/Publications/ Medialaw/fairelect.htm* [accessed 8 January 2009]

Election Day Reporting

Once the polling stations have opened, the role of the mass media changes considerably from that of the campaign period. Specific rules may be devised to govern this shift. In practice, the shift may have taken place earlier, with embargoes placed on political campaign reporting, opinion poll reporting, direct-access broadcasts or advertisements. The implications for a ban on reporting during the polls are more complex, depending on the length of the voting exercise and size of the country.

Similarly, voting across multiple time zones poses serious challenges, as results from one time zone may become available before voting has closed in another. In essence, it is important to preserve the integrity of the electoral process and the security of the vote, and to ensure that untimely release of information does not influence the vote.

It is often difficult to strike a balance between allowing the media some sort of special access to report on the voting process, while at the same time ensuring that voters' secrecy and security are not breached. An obsession with security usually leads to discomfort and even confrontation between the media and security forces during some parts of the voting process.

Promoting Professional Coverage of Results

In principle, covering results sounds like the least complicated part of the whole election reporting process. Yet, remarkably, this is often the area where the media performs poorest. In Zimbabwe's referendum of 2000, for instance, not a single newspaper or broadcasting station reported the results issued by the Registrar General's Office accurately. The Zimbabwe situation was to be repeated spectacularly in the US elections in 2004, when the media had its figures confused.

Most problems in this area are attributable to the media itself. If journalists cannot copy a column of data correctly, or they interpret such data inaccurately, there is little that the election administrator can do. Much can be done to promote accurate and professional results reporting. Providing a central location where media can gain access to official information related to the elections (a media centre) will facilitate media access to results enormously. While counting mechanisms may vary enormously between centralised and decentralised systems, the significant point for the purposes of media reporting is whether results are released centrally or locally. If the latter, media reporting will also need to be decentralised.

Where a system of local counting is implemented, as for example in the United Kingdom, an elaborate media machine has evolved for projecting a final tally from the available results. In Zimbabwe's March 2008 presidential elections, parallel vote tabulation – unofficial tabulation of official local results – was implemented. This is a serious and important way to prevent vote fraud. 'Quick counts'[25] – defined by the US National Democratic Institute (NDI) as a method whereby observers watch the voting and counting processes at selected polling stations, record key information on standardised forms and report their findings to a data collection centre – were also used in the Philippines (1987), Chile (1988), Zambia (2001), Ghana (1996) and Pakistan (2007, 2008) as part of efforts to limit official malfeasance. They were aggressively marketed to the media as a counterforce to fraud in vote tallying. NDI says quick count methodology is also used to evaluate the overall quality of election-day processes and to verify official election results.[26]

What is of primary importance when results emerge gradually is that they are reported promptly and accurately. Doing so is an important media function, since it provides a means of public scrutiny of the counting process and reduces the possibility of fraudulent manipulation. A different aspect of results reporting is the coverage of projected results in the form of exit polls.[27]

Having chastised Zimbabwe for the chaotic reporting of the 2000 referendum, it has to be noted that great improvement was made in the 2008 parliamentary election. The main reason for this was that the Zimbabwe Electoral Commission (ZEC) allowed local election officials to post the result at constituency headquarters – and the media therefore had just one result to report per constituency. The same formula appeared to work for the first round of the presidential elections until, midway through the process, the ZEC suspended the posting of elections and withheld official results for a month – irreversibly undermining the credibility of the official result.

Post-Election Reporting

Media interest in an election does not stop with the results announcement. It is a continuing story that leads on to the inauguration of the newly elected, selection of a new government and turns in an audit of a candidate or government's first 100 days in office. For the election authority, however, any formal media regulation ends with the announcement. It is to be noted that formal media involvement may continue if results are challenged, in which case coverage should adhere to professional standards governing reporting of court proceedings.

Tony Fraser – Trinidad and Tobago

The first requirement of a journalist covering an election in Trinidad and Tobago is to understand the multicultural nature and culture of the people, the disposition to exaggeration of politicians and political parties, the apparent contradictions of the culture and to vow not take the country's politics too seriously. At the same time, however, the journalist must appreciate that vital ethnic and cultural superiority and economic survival are riding on the outcome of the polls. Every general election in Trinidad and Tobago in the last 15 years has been deemed the 'Mother of all election battles'.

Why are the elections so absolutely crucial yet comically flawed? Because the political economy and culture are divided absolutely along ethnic lines. The two major political parties, indeed cultures, are stratified along the lines of the Afro-Trinidadian population – 39 per cent of the country's 1.3 million population have their ancestry in Africa – and the Indo-Trinidadian 41 per cent segment of the country that originated in India, their ancestors having been brought to the country between 1845–1917 as immigrants to work in the sugar cane plantations owned by British settlers. The remaining 20 per cent of the population consists of people with their ancestry in Europe, the Middle East (Jew and Arab alike), China and a bewildering array of people of mixed ancestry born to the free inter-mixing and marrying of the above people.

The understanding of this plural society by the journalist allows him or her to appreciate that – notwithstanding the mixed population and the free intermingling and inter-racial solidarity that exist amongst the groups – when it comes to politics and elections, the source of cultural and financial power, the population is divided along ethnic lines.

As the calypsonian, the chronicler of the culture, has sung: 'how we party, is not how we vote'. Calypsonian, David Rudder, makes the point in song that while people mix freely with no geographical or ethnic separation, they vote along ethnic lines, much as their parties are based along those lines rather than ideological or programmatic bases. But as confusing as it may be, the journalist must understand that no matter how tribalised the voting patterns, increasingly and with continuing growth in the mixed population, election outcomes are being determined by the mixed population voting in what have come to be known as 'marginal constituencies'. These comprise four of five electoral districts, in which the mixed population has what amounts to a casting vote when the two tribes are locked together in terms of numbers of votes: here, it is the choice of the mixed population that separates and makes the difference.

The use by political leaders of deep ethnic codes, including language and symbols of groups, is quite telling. Deciphering the codes can be a challenge to the reporter. Moreover, the question always arises whether reporting and explaining the codes could foster ethnic antagonism and further divide the society. Another approach would be to consider that reporting the coded language would unmask the politicians and their intentions. The journalist covering the elections in Trinidad and Tobago must also appreciate and be able to convey (especially to an external audience) that notwithstanding the predominance of Afro-Trinis and Indo-Trinis separately in the two major political parties, the Indo party also contains large numbers of Afros and people of mixed origin and vice versa for the Afro party, which also contains Indos and those of mixed ethnicities. This could be confusing, having already neatly categorised the parties along lines of ethnicity.

To get the 'A–Z' of covering an election right, the journalist must understand, and factor into the coverage, the country's song and dance culture with the accompanying food and drink: during one period, it was referred to as 'Rum and Roti Politics' – a favourite drink and food of the national culture. Election campaigns are virtual open-air parties of music, dance and celebration almost as in victory, which take place every night in the political meetings during the campaigns. Moreover, the party-like atmosphere pervades the platforms of speakers as much as it does the crowds. The music, a mixture of calypso, which is the national song (although it originates from the Afro-Trini population) and the chutney, the Indian blend of music in the Caribbean, plus a touch of reggae, the Jamaican music made famous by Bob Marley, fills the evenings with live performances by artists who carry part of the parties' messages in song on stage.

In the last week of the campaigns, the major meetings cross over into full-fledged carnival celebrations approximating the pre-Lenten festival, which Trinidad and Tobago is most famous for and which nationals boast to be 'The Greatest Show on Earth', without apology to the Brazilian samba variety of carnival.

The discerning journalist, fully aware of the political culture, will treat the 'carnivals' seriously and look for the messages and sub-text in song and dance and have his/her copy, video and sound reflect those messages as part of the 'A-Z' of elections coverage in Trinidad and Tobago. Covering the election and giving it its full flavour and meaning is not merely to create excitement for readers, viewers and listeners, but because so much of the communication of the culture is wrapped-up in the national cultures of the multi-ethnic, religious and cultural society. As colourful as the culture surrounding the

> 'Covering the political campaign also requires the journalist to be aware of repetition, as the major political figures carry into their five to six week campaigns one basic speech adapted and added and taken away from as the nights proceed.'
>
> Tony Fraser
> Broadcast journalist

meetings is, so too are the political figures and their speeches, tending to being verbose, full of 'robber talk' – grand declarations, challenges and policy positions, many of which are unconnected to reality. 'Robber talk' is the grandiloquent speech pattern of an historical character of the Carnival called the Midnight Robber, who assails the audience with his imaginary criminal deeds, all pure flights of fancy. Political leaders place themselves in the tradition of the Midnight Robber to give themselves an aura of invincibility to supporters and those who would gravitate to them.

Covering the political campaign also requires the journalist to be aware of repetition, as the major political figures carry into their five to six week campaigns one basic speech adapted and added and taken away from as the nights proceed. The demands are therefore on the journalist to find the new, newsworthy elements of the speeches to convey to readers, viewers and listeners. Here, too, the reporter on the election trail must be alive to responses to the contentions coming from the platform of the other party. Covering the campaigns requires also that the journalist undertakes quite an amount of research on the statements/claims of the parties and their leaders, to find the contradictions and past failures of those making claims to achieve re-stated objectives. Also of vital importance is discernment and follow-up encounters with political figures in more sober news conferences, to source new stories and analytical features in order to make the audience fully aware of the history of the claims, counter claims, failed policies etc. Such research must also focus on the manifesto proposals of the parties, as they very rarely make it to the political campaign, being considered without sufficient allure for the party-type atmosphere that prevails at meetings.

And this is all required notwithstanding the reality that journalists like all others come from the ethnic groups involved, and have been nurtured in the political culture like everyone else. The political culture is quite unforgiving of the journalist who takes a side, notwithstanding the fact that supporters of each party are unapologetically biased to one side or the other.[28]

Commonwealth Observer Group report

The Gambia Election, 2006

Note: *Three main parties contested the election. They were the Alliance For Patriotic Re-Orientation and Construction (APRC) of President Yahya Jammeh; the coalition comprising the United Democratic Party (UDP), National Reconciliation Party (NRP) and Gambian People's Democratic Party; and the National Alliance for Democracy and Development coalition (NADD). This election followed a period of instability in The Gambia, which included an attempted coup against President Jammeh's government in March 2006.*

Overview

There are both public and private media in The Gambia. The print media in operation during the election period were the *Daily Observer* and *The Point*, which are The Gambia's daily newspapers. The weekly papers are *Forayaa* and the *Gambia News and Reports*. The Gambia Radio and Television Services (GRTS) are government-owned. Other radio stations in operation were West Coast and City Limits. Most radio stations are localised and mainly broadcast in local languages.

In 2002, under the Media Law, a Commission was set up with powers ranging from issuing licenses to prosecuting journalists. Freedom of the press and intimidation of journalists have been issues of concern in The Gambia. The private media faced restraints and threats of high license fees leading into the election. This was seen by critics and media professionals as a threat to freedom of speech.

Further legislation introduced in late-2004 provided jail terms for journalists found guilty of libel or sedition. Deyda Hydara, one of the press law's leading critics and editor of *The Point*, a private newspaper, was shot dead days after the law was passed. There have been calls for a public enquiry into this matter.

The media code of conduct

During the 2006 Presidential Election, media coverage of the campaign period was guided by a code of conduct that was developed by the media with support from the Independent Elections Commission (IEC). In this regard the public medium, which includes GRTS, was required to provide fair access for all political parties and candidates. Section 78 of the Elections Decree stipulated that the IEC should ensure that 'equal airtime is given to each candidate and national party on the public radio and television'. The television station provided 30 minutes coverage of political rally activity reports per party per day, and 10 minutes of direct broadcast access to voters per party per day. GRTS covered news, with content line-up being primarily pro-government.

Media monitoring findings

The IEC contracted an independent consultant to monitor media coverage of the electoral process. The media monitored were: GRTS TV and GRTS Radio; the *Daily Observer*, *The Point*, and *Forayaa* newspapers; and West Coast FM and Kids with Talent FM radio stations.

Some of the general findings of the IEC contracted Media Monitoring Unit conducted from 5-15 September 2006 were that:

- Political rallies regulated access on GRTS TV showed a clear advantage to APRC

- GRTS TV did not broadcast the IEC political platform regulated access programmes, at least at a convenient hour

- Newscasts on GRTS TV gave overwhelming precedence to APRC, but also mentioned UDP and NADD

- Newscasts on GRTS Radio were more equitable between APRC and NADD, but did not mention UDP

- Private radio stations did not carry a minimum five minutes coverage of the election, as required by the Elections Decree

- There was no direct negative portrayal (in context and presentation) on GRTS radio and television

- The print media was intensely covering the candidates' campaigns

The group noted that private radio stations did not adequately report on the campaign, but covered other social and entertainment programmes. Some media analysts told the group that 'politics and elections were dangerous subject to cover' and that they instead chose to cover 'safe subjects'.

GRTS Television gave overwhelmingly favourable coverage to the APRC party throughout the campaign period, especially during the Prime News hour at 8.00pm. This finding was corroborated by the group from a sample of the newscasts that were watched.

Commonwealth Observer Group report

Zambia Election, 2006

Note: *Zambia's 2006 election was a three-way affair between the ruling Movement for Multiparty Democracy of incumbent President Levy Patrick Mwanawasa, the United Party for National Development led by businessman Anderson Mazoka and the Patriotic Front of former cabinet minister Michael Sata. It was the third democratic election since the end of one-party rule in 1990.*

Media

... The 2006 Electoral Code of Conduct contains provisions in regard to 'Duties of the Media', 'Allocation of Airtime', and 'Election Results Programme'. These include the requirement that 'all print and electronic media shall provide fair and balanced reporting of the campaigns, policies, meetings, rallies and press conferences of all registered political parties and candidates during the period of campaigning'. This and other requirements appear to outlaw media bias and to promote a level media playing field for all candidates. However, these provisions were not always rigorously enforced.

Two provisions of the code met with resistance from media practitioners. One provided that 'all public and private media personnel shall ... refrain from broadcasting their own political commentary or assessment; and where they wish to do so, they shall clearly identify the opinion, commentary or assessment as their own and shall carefully balance it in order to avoid bias'. The other provided that the media 'shall not speculate election results, but shall broadcast confirmed election results as they are announced by presiding officers'. These were felt by some journalists to inhibit freedom of expression, but were defended by the ECZ [Electoral Commission of Zambia] as the most appropriate and responsible way of making public the outcome of the elections.

There are in Zambia both state-owned and private media, and we observed no restriction on media freedom. Estimates of the reach of print and broadcast media suggest that some 70 per cent of the population is influenced primarily by radio, and 30 per cent primarily by the print media. The general impression was that there had been significant improvement in the performance of the media as compared with the 2001 elections. However, there was still evidence of bias towards the ruling party on the part of the government-controlled media, in terms of news coverage of the campaign.

The print and broadcast media were also used for voter education, including in local languages. The code of conduct was extensively advertised in the press by the ECZ. Newspapers carried editorials and articles on the importance of turning out to vote. Voter education information sponsored by the ECZ and civil society organisations was disseminated on television and radio. Most voter education information was of high quality, urging registered voters to cast their vote on polling day, and giving reasons why it was important for Zambians to exercise their voting rights. Some of this was targeted specifically at young people.

Our observers did not attempt a systematic quantitative analysis of the elections-related media coverage, but rather carried out a sampling of the media as available to them. Our observations are, however, largely borne out by the analysis done by other observer missions.

The print media

Zambia has three national daily newspapers: the *Zambia Daily Mail* and the *Times of Zambia* are government-owned, while *The Post* is owned by several private shareholders, including some politicians. There are also three weekly papers.

During the election period, some efforts were made towards balanced coverage by most of the news media. The government majority-owned newspapers generally devoted considerably more coverage to the ruling party, and coverage of the incumbent's campaign was positive in tone. Coverage of opposition candidates and parties was more limited and sometimes appeared to foreshadow negative consequences if one of the opposition parties were to win. The news coverage of *The Post* was more balanced, providing access to the three leading presidential candidates. However, the tone was more frequently negative for both ruling party and opposition candidates.

The group received complaints from some opposition parties about pro-government bias in the print media. For example, the Ndola branch of PF complained to our observers that its press releases and denials of allegations made by the ruling party seldom got printed.

Both public and private newspapers carried political party advertising for the leading presidential candidates and their parties. Some of this was however negative in tone, seeking to imply that if a particular political party won, there would be negative repercussions for the people and the nation.

On the day before polling, the *Times of Zambia* included a supplement consisting of two full-page advertisements for MMD, together with the code of conduct. We do not believe that it was appropriate for these to appear together in the same supplement.

Reporting on the results process was fairly balanced. On Saturday 30 September, while results were still being tallied and announced, *The Post* headline was 'Levy headed for victory', while the *Zambia Daily Mail* led with 'Sata maintains grip'. The *Times* headline was 'MMD, PF in tight race'. The following day, the *Times* and *Mail* said that Mr Mwanawasa was now ahead, while *The Post* said 'I've won by 55% – Sata'.

Electronic media

The Zambian National Broadcasting Corporation is the state-owned broadcaster, operating the only nationally available television channel, as well as three radio stations (Radios 1, 2 and 4). Privately owned radio stations broadcast in various parts of the country. Radio Phoenix and Radio Christian Voice have coverage in several regions. There are also community radio stations broadcasting over a smaller radius in many regions. However, in some of the more remote rural areas, very little radio broadcasting was accessible.

ZNBC displayed a worrying degree of bias in its news reportage of the campaign, with almost all campaign-related images and most of its verbal reportage devoted to the incumbent president. The first four or five items on the news would typically be on the President's speech at various functions or meetings. Meanwhile, coverage of opposition rallies, where provided, was mainly much shorter in duration, without pictures but often including negative news such as alleged logistical failings or negative statements allegedly made by speakers.

According to some stakeholders, this bias in favour of the incumbent was unavoidable because he remained the President, and needed to continue his official functions. It was argued that it was difficult to draw a clear line between official and party functions, and the news coverage was simply presenting information on what the government had done and proposed to do. A further argument presented to the group was that ZNBC had a limited number of cameras and reporters and they naturally tended to give preference to the President's functions and therefore to such coverage in the news.

We were informed that the ECZ had summoned the ZNBC and informed them that their news coverage contravened the code of conduct. This produced a short-term improvement in the balance of ZNBC's television coverage. However, the improvement was temporary and the pro-government bias returned after a few days.

The majority of paid advertising for presidential candidates was also in favour of the ruling party. This included some negative advertising about the PF candidate, which ZNBC persisted in broadcasting despite the party concerned having obtained a High Court injunction ordering ZNBC to desist.

Media coverage sponsored by ECZ and the Zambia Chapter of the Media Institute of Southern Africa (MISA) was balanced and equitable. Time was given to all presidential candidates to convey their manifestos. Parliamentary candidates from the various parties were also given time to discuss and debate. However, one opposition party complained that broadcasting of their presidential candidate's message coincided with a power blackout in the Central Province.

There is also an issue regarding the ZNBC Act in regard to the appointment of the Board of

Directors. The law requires the Minister of Information to submit to Parliament for its approval a proposal for the appointment of the Board of Directors. Media organisations such MISA and the Press Association of Zambia petitioned the court that the government had not acted in accordance with the law. The court ruled in the media organisations' favour, but the government appealed to the Supreme Court. A final decision was postponed until after the election period.

Overall assessment

Our overall assessment is that considerable progress has been made in Zambia in terms of freedom to campaign, freedom of expression and in the level of balance in media coverage of the election campaign.

However, there remains room for improvement regarding the use of state resources in election campaigns and the news coverage of the campaign by the state-owned electronic media. Alleged breaches of the code of conduct in this regard should be vigorously investigated.

Correct application of the ZNBC Act and the implementation of proposals to establish an independent broadcasting authority should also help to improve political balance in the broadcasting media.

4 New Communication Technologies

In the recent past, new media has played an important role in both controlling and expanding democratic space. This phenomenon seems to have had a significant impact on recent elections in transition democracies such as Kenya. Most new media forms are emerging from the Internet and mobile (cellular) telephones.

For societies emerging from years of single-party rule, a common dilemma for the fledgling political opposition has been how to mobilise supporters given the ruling party's domination of the normal channels of communication. Hence, new political campaigning strategies have emerged in response, including online chain-mail,[29] campaigns through mobile phone text messaging and the use of cell phones to mobilise supporters into action. These methods open up a communication space that is beyond the reach of the traditional mass media. Given these developments, it is abundantly clear that traditional campaign regulations need to be updated to cover emerging forms of telecommunications.

New Interactive Media

Modern political campaigns in transition democracies tend to embrace what is happening in developed democracies. With the advent of cable communication, mobile telephony, satellite television and the proliferation of private broadcasting, political campaigns have intensified to such an extent that a new political communication culture is evolving. Yet existing practices and principles of media behaviour in elections were largely developed for what is now regarded to be 'old' media: newspapers, radio and television. Some of these have been overtaken by the emergent new forms of media.

New communication technologies offer numerous positive opportunities for the electoral process itself. These include voter registration (and even voting) via the Internet or cell phone. This is in addition to the role that these technologies could play as news or campaigning media. In any event, many assumptions that underpin the regulation of conventional media do not apply to new media. For example, the World Wide Web ('the

Web') has infinite space to publish material, yet the assumption behind broadcasting regulation is that the frequency spectrum is a finite resource that must be shared.

New technologies also help to challenge the dominance of powerful corporate or governmental voices in the media. It is far easier for individuals or small groups to set up websites or send text messages on cell phones than it is to launch newspapers or television stations. Internet and other new communication technologies are carried on media (such as telephone lines) owned by governments or large corporations, but this obstacle can be circumvented through direct broadcasts or satellite reception.

The main regulatory challenge posed by new media is that, unlike old media, it can only be regulated in ways that constitute censorship or restrict freedom of expression. Some common regulatory actions include interception of emails, closure of websites, disabling of text message services, and pressure or legal action against Internet service providers. This compares to the judicial measures usually used to regulate 'old media'.

The diverse reach of new media deserves further mention, especially its radical challenge to traditional views of media conduct during elections. Election reporting blackouts, for example, have been rendered virtually obsolete by the activities of unregulated websites. At the same time, the global nature of the Internet renders its content beyond regulation by national electoral authorities. Attempts by regulators to close down websites are met by the creation of mirror sites (replicas) beyond the country's borders. Analysts caution that this regulatory challenge could rapidly extend beyond the written word, to Internet radio and television. Already new variants such as podcasting (the broadcasting of audio materials over the Internet), Really Simple Syndication (RSS)[30] and peer-to-peer networks have taken root.

Because Internet services are still beyond the reach of a majority of people in developing countries, one might be tempted to ask: why does it matter? Yet where the 'elite' work as the information agency of a village, one Internet connection or one mobile telephone receiving a text (also known as a SMS or short message service) can inform the entire community.

Communications Revolution

Researchers and journalists agree that cell phones are the platform of now and the future. In his paper 'Mobile Phones, Identity and

Discursive Intimacy', technology scholar Raul Pertierra (2005) asserts that recent trends suggest that cell phones are increasingly taking a major role in this communications revolution.

The interconnectivity of mobile telephony, computers, radio, television and print media are producing new communication structures, with often-unpredictable consequences. New media will bring about important social changes, from personal identity to political mobilisation, and from virtual spaces or simulated models to lived realities and embodied geographies. It is hoped that the new media may also assist in the gathering and dissemination of alternative information sources, creating virtual public spaces where citizens can debate vital issues and organise appropriate political action.

Pertierra, citing elections in the Philippines, says the cell phone was important in co-ordinating the movement of candidates and their supporters, as well as in the government's keeping a close watch on the activities of the political opposition. Pertierra argued that events such as weddings, baptisms, burials and senior citizens' meetings always draw large crowds and candidates made sure that they were present, and importantly that the cell phone played an important role in keeping track of these activities.[31] In the 2007 Sierra Leone presidential elections, journalists despatched their stories from rural districts to editors in the capital Freetown via SMS and observer groups, including one from the Commonwealth Secretariat, convened news conferences by sending text messages to media hotlines or political reporters.[32]

The Internet and Elections

The Internet has been hailed as the next revolution in electoral communications, just as it is claimed to have revolutionised the global flow of information. Opinion polls are already conducted via the Internet, although these are still seriously unreliable. In a context where the conventional media is highly censored, the Internet can be an important means for small numbers of people to receive politically sensitive information, which can then be more widely circulated. In other words, for most of the globe, the significance of the Internet is more that it will enable alternative ideas to be put into circulation, rather than it serving as a means of mass communication by parties, candidates or electoral authorities.

The 'convergence' between broadcasting and telecommunications – telephony has moved towards the use of satellites, while broadcasting has moved towards the use of fibre-optic cable – is also likely to lead to a closer linkage between traditional media and the Internet.

The Internet has become a major campaign tool for political groups. The United States provides the best example of high-tech, Internet-based fundraising where, for example, US President Barack Obama raised millions of dollars via the medium for his successful campaign.

At the same time, Internet campaigning is gaining currency among the educated elite and young people in developing countries, including in Africa. However, the medium is still limited by poverty and to some extent the reluctance of politicians – especially those who have been on the stage right from the independence era, who are cultured in the principle of 'strong-man leadership' rather than the possibility of spontaneous interaction with the electorate. Politicians' websites tend to carry the same material as that that is available in other traditional formats.

One other area of election-related Internet development is activism by NGOs. In the United States, election activism includes searchable online databases on financial contributions to the different candidates' campaigns or on a candidate's voting record. If applied honestly and accurately, these developments can only enhance democracy. A more problematic development, however, is the use of Internet reporting to subvert conventions that have been widely accepted by 'traditional' media, for example, reporting exit polls before voting has ended.

An important characteristic of the Internet is the ease of access for individuals and small organisations. For instance, the medium has lowered costs associated with traditional publishing (although the problem of quality control still exists). Lowered costs have also led to the emergence of 'blogging' (a contraction of the term 'web log'). These independent and often intemperate individual diaries ('blogs') have been condemned and praised in equal measure. Regardless, they are a political phenomenon that is here to stay.

Other technological developments within the Internet will also have political ramifications. The Really Simple Syndication (RSS news feeds) discussed above provide a means of disseminating news stories rapidly and at virtually no cost. Web video sites such as *YouTube* and peer-to-peer networks allow the simple, low-cost transfer of large files (such as audio and video files) to a wide audience. 'Podcasting' is a term coined to describe the broadcasting of audio materials over the Internet (and in theory their downloading to personal media players or for re-broadcast by local or community radio stations).

The Internet can also be an important way of distributing broadcast signals through streaming. This is a particularly effective way of making programming available to local or regional radio stations in large countries. Indonesia recently experimented with this approach, and reported a high potential for distributing voter education material or direct-access slots.

Mobile Phones and Elections

As earlier mentioned, wireless communication and cell phones are becoming increasingly widespread. In addition to voice calling, cell phones are a platform for new services such as text messaging, email and basic Internet browsing, all of which are potentially useful to the election process.

For instance, until recently home computers in Japan were considered the province of *otaku* (reclusive, obsessive intellectuals). Cell phones, on the other hand, have long been extremely popular and the primary interface of most Japanese users to email and the Internet. Cell phones also have special relevance for countries with a poor, fixed telephone infrastructure. Radio is by far the most dominant medium in Africa, and the recent proliferation of independent radio stations and cellular infrastructure is already affecting politics. In the run up to Ghana's December 2000 elections, radio phone-in shows pilloried the hand-picked successor of Jerry Rawlings, the outgoing president. The candidate, John Atta Mills, lost the election. During the election itself, voters used cell phones and talk radio to report voting fraud.

Two factors support common arguments that mobile phones are an important medium for electoral communication. First, ownership and access to cellular phones far outstrips that of fixed landlines. This disparity is especially apparent in poorer countries, but it is now a general phenomenon. Second, cell phones have potential as a 'broadcasting' medium that is incomparable to traditional landlines. While landlines could be used for voice and fax communications, cell phones can send and receive text messages, data audio and even video files.

The use of cell phones in political campaigning or broadcasting may not be fully developed, but the potential is obvious and is growing rapidly. The Philippines offers two well-documented examples. In 2001, a popular campaign against President Joseph Estrada was orchestrated by SMS, forcing him to resign. Then, in the 2004 presidential elections, texting proved to be a popular campaigning tool for the main candidates.[33]

It is hard to see how SMS could easily be brought within the regulatory ambit without resorting to heavy-handed censorship. Another concern is that text messaging, like email, can easily be 'spoofed'. This means that messages can be sent from masked or fake addresses (as with email 'spam' or junk mail), making the regulator's task even more difficult. Yet characteristics that make regulation difficult can also be positive: in the Zimbabwe elections in 2008, SMS was about the only major tool available to the opposition parties, as the country's mass media – owned by the government – offered limited or no coverage of opposition messages.

What has so far been confined to SMS could rapidly develop through audio and video files, with the development of 'third generation' (3G) phones capable of exchanging such files easily. This is where Internet-based techniques like podcasting and cellular telephony overlap. Political broadcasts could be distributed by a mixture of media, to be watched or listened to on telephones or personal stereo players. These technologies are potentially available to all players in election campaigns. Parties can use them to distribute campaign material, the media can use them to increase audience numbers and electoral managers can use them to educate voters and increase political participation. Indeed, President Barack Obama did exactly this during his 2008 election campaign.

Civil society groups and political parties have also experimented with text messaging to prevent elections fraud in the wake of the botched Kenya (2007) and Zimbabwe (2008) elections. In Ghana's December 2008 elections, NGOs under the umbrella group the Coalition of Domestic Election Observers (CODEO) used mobile phones to hinder the potential falsifying of results. According to the *Financial Times*:

> *The system works like this: volunteers with mobile phones monitor a representative sample of 1,000 out of some 21,000 polling*

stations. As voting gets under way, they send text messages containing data on the conduct in their polling station to a toll-free number. A cheat-sheet lists the codes. For example, a text containing 'D1' means 'ballot box missing'. Mobile-based schemes have been used to monitor votes in Indonesia, Montenegro, Egypt and Sierra Leone in recent years, but the developers say Ghana has the most sophisticated version yet deployed. CODEO volunteers hope the SMS-based scheme can be replicated elsewhere to prevent incumbents leaning on electoral officials to bump up their tallies.[34]

TESTIMONY

Joyce Mulama – Kenya

Kenya held its last elections in December 2007 and
the violence that followed them is well documented.
Severe deficiencies within the electoral process and the
sheer incompetence of the Electoral Commission of
Kenya (ECK) have also been documented in a detailed
manner by a Judicial Review Commission, which was
created as part of a power-sharing agreement between
the main political parties that contested that election
– the Party of National Unity fronted by President
Mwai Kibaki and the Orange Democratic Movement of Raila Odinga, who took the post
of Prime Minister in a political arrangement designed to end further bloodshed.

I will discuss a number of issues relevant to the electoral process in Kenya, focusing
specifically on the pre-disputed results and period of violence period in the country.
Because of the sensitivity of the subject, the importance of upholding high standards
of objectivity in election reporting cannot be overemphasised. Politicians and political
parties, however weak, expect not to be sidelined in terms of coverage. Yet, in the
Kenyan situation, a number of media houses have been known to take visible sides.
While it can be stated that over the years the mainstream media has become stronger
and has demonstrated objective coverage of elections, the tabloid press – or the pink
and yellow pages as they are better known in Kenya – has bent the rules of objective
reporting and taken sides many times, rarely veiling their opinions. The reason
sometimes lies in the fact that politicians own some of the tabloids and use them as
propaganda tools. On a more positive note, however, the larger population pays more
attention to the mainstream media, reading the 'gutter press' mostly for the
entertainment that scandals and occasional heresy provide.

Timely information is of the essence in election coverage, from a moral viewpoint so
that it may calm peoples' often-extreme anxiety, and on the commercial side to get to
the market before the competition. All the mainstream electronic media have recently
acquired equipment to enable them to present live coverage of events. This is already
being applied in campaigns coverage, and boosted viewers during the elections in
December 2007. Such swift information flow, together with an objective electoral
commission, is known to have played a role before in frustrating attempts to falsify
results of elections. In this respect, I have in mind the 2002 elections, when the Electoral
Commission of Kenya chairman, Samuel Kivuitu, told the media, including myself, that
the government was attempting to rig the election. His forthrightness and ensuing

prompt media coverage, in addition to the greater vigilance by the opposition his statement generated, probably saved the day. Unfortunately, following the 2007 elections, he was quoted as saying he did not know whether President Mwai Kibaki had won, casting a huge shadow on the process. Mr Kivuitu later clarified that his statement had been taken out of context, and he actually meant he did not know whether the President had won 'fairly'. But the damage had already been done.

With live coverage comes the possibility of libel suits, because journalists seldom have much time to edit what will be broadcast. Hence, there is the need for extreme caution in this manner of reporting, despite the prompt coverage it allows of important events. Nonetheless, the greatest challenge of providing information quickly comes with the inaccessibility of remote areas, where even telephone network coverage is absent (unless media houses invest in costly satellite telephony). Network coverage notwithstanding, mobile phones have proved effective in ensuring the swift flow of information. During the 2002 elections, journalists covering them would monitor proceedings, including vote-counting results in different locations, by calling or sending short text messages to each other. This meant they were able to pass on the same information to their respective media houses, which in turn would relay the information to the public.

> 'Politicians and political parties, however weak, expect not to be sidelined in terms of coverage. Yet, in the Kenyan situation, a number of media houses have been known to take visible sides.'
>
> Joyce Mulama

Kenyan mainstream media now encourages opinion pieces written by outside commentators. The challenge here is to ensure that such contributions, which are often written by non journalists, remain objective. Recent suspicions are that some regular commentators are on the payroll of politicians or political parties, and bend their opinions to suit certain interests. These writers veil their support for specific parties and individuals, providing politicians with another track to astutely penetrate the media and gain mileage. Fortunately, the mainstream media is now alert on such attempts, and has blacklisted some personalities in recent years.

In order to sustain good electoral coverage, the journalist-led Media Council of Kenya holds workshops aimed at equipping journalists with election-reporting skills. The ECK also conducts similar seminars for media players, telling them to exercise caution during electioneering periods. In time it is hoped more objectivity will be exercised and legal procedures observed, raising the standards of elections reportage in Kenya.

Election coverage requires that the journalist is knowledgeable about the area he or she has been assigned to cover. This means that the reporter must engage in research on the politics of the area, the voting patterns, the number of registered voters etc., in order to be able to provide the right information and analysis. Covering elections is as complex and adventurous as it is challenging. Below are some of the underlying hurdles faced by journalist when covering elections in Kenya:

- **Denial by politicians of statements attributed to them**, especially once they realise they have made a mistake. They tend to turn on the reporter and accuse him/her of having a hidden agenda, of 'misquoting' or quoting them 'out of context', regardless of whether they were caught on tape or not.

- **Intimidation by politicians alone or by politicians and their supporters.** This obstacle particularly affects regional (upcountry) correspondents, especially when they are filing stories by phone on location. There have been cases of supporters of particular candidates besieging reporters filing stories in this manner, to make sure they (the reporters) do not criticise their favourite candidate. For example, at a campaign rally just before the 2002 elections, a female parliamentary aspirant was seriously assaulted by alleged supporters of her competitor. The assailants then threatened the journalists covering the event (myself included), confiscated our cameras and recorders, and left us to run for our lives.

- **Offers to be the 'media eye' of particular candidates,** to ensure any negative stories about those candidates are quashed. Journalists have been offered large sums of monies to play such roles, and the pressure can be overbearing to the extent that some (usually reporters on low incomes) give in and start taking sides.

- **Being caught up in the midst of election violence.** Violent youth have in the past often vented their anger on journalists covering events. This happened on a number of occasions in the run up to the 2007 elections.

- **The risk of being violently thrown out of a political rally** for reporting on behalf of a particular media house, especially when the organisers are unhappy with that media organisation for 'not supporting' their cause. In other words, some politicians may expect a journalist to support their agenda (perhaps because they share the same neighbourhood or ethnicity) to the extent that the journalist is vilified (sometimes publicly) when he or she refuses and remains objective.

- Another challenge is **the fatigue often associated with elections coverage.** Vote counting takes place by hand and journalists must witness the process to completion.

- **Accessing remote areas,** where roads are terrible or even non-existent. How many media houses can hire helicopters to follow politicians flying in the same? Often, journalists are provided with transport by politicians, but how fair is their reporting going to be about the person who is responsible for their travel?[35]

Commonwealth Observer Group report

Malawi Election, 2004

Note: *There are more than 30 registered political parties in Malawi, although only 15 of these took part in the elections, with two broad alliances. The ruling United Democratic Front (UDF) was in alliance with the Alliance for Democracy (AFORD) and the New Congress for Democracy (NCD). The opposition Mgwirizano Coalition comprised the Republican Party, the People's Progressive Movement (PPM), Malawi Forum for Unity and Development (Mafunde), Malawi Democratic Party (MDP), National Unity Party, Movement for Genuine Democratic Change (MGODE) and the People's Transformation Party. Other parties which participated in the election were the Malawi Congress Party (MCP), National Democratic Alliance (NDA), Congress for National Unity (CONU), National Solidarity Movement (NSM) and Pamodzi Freedom Party (PFP).*

There were five Presidential candidates: Mr Gwanda Chakuamba Mgwirizano (Coalition), Mr Justin Malewezi (Independent), Mr Brown Mpinganjira (National Democratic Alliance), Dr Bingu wa Mutharika (UDF/AFORD/NCD) and Mr John Tembo (Malawi Congress Party). A total of 1,258 candidates contested the 193 parliamentary seats, including 373 independents.

Media

Ten years into multi-party democracy, the media in Malawi has diversified. The country now has a small but vigorous privately owned press and a handful of commercial radio stations. But the state-run Malawi Broadcasting Corporation (MBC) radio station, established in 1964, dominates the airwaves, as well as public broadcaster Television Malawi (TVM), which was set up in 1999; and the legacy of the country's first 30 years of one-party rule still shapes the information sector to an unhealthy degree.

None of the information outlets were without fault, but MBC radio deserves to be singled out for critical comment. It is the main, if not the sole, source of information for the majority of voters. This is why its responsibilities are set out in the Parliamentary and Presidential Elections Act (1993). Part V Section 63 (1) states that: 'Every political party shall have the right to have the substance of its campaign propaganda reported on radio news broadcasts of the Malawi Broadcasting Corporation and in any newspapers in circulation in Malawi.' Yet in the run-up to the 2004 election, MBC radio and TVM failed to meet the statutory terms and news output almost exclusively reflected the views of the ruling alliance.

Three decades of one-party rule under the first independent government of the Malawi Congress Party (MCP), which ruled from 1964 to 1994, have been instrumental in the conduct of the state-run media to date. Since 1994, with the transition of power from the

MCP to the ruling UDF/AFORD alliance, the media monopoly has given way to allow the entry of private radio stations and newspapers. But the ruling coalition has continued to use the state media – MBC radio and TVM – for propaganda and political campaigns.

There have been many changes in all information sectors – newspapers, radio and television – since the first democratic elections in 1994 (when Commonwealth observers were last present) and the 1999 elections (which were assessed by a team from the Commonwealth Secretariat). The emergence of privately owned press and radio after decades of dominance by state-controlled media is undoubtedly a positive development, and one of the fruits of democracy.

> The emergence of privately owned press and radio after decades of dominance by state-controlled media is undoubtedly a positive development, and one of the fruits of democracy.

Radio

MBC radio remains the main source of news for the 70 to 80 per cent of Malawians who live in rural areas. Many cannot afford to buy a newspaper and, even if they could, newspapers are rarely available outside urban areas. Low literacy levels are a further barrier.

In terms of the level of coverage, MBC radio remains the most important medium of communication, followed by private radio stations (most of which are limited to the capital Lilongwe, Blantyre and Mzuzu), TVM and newspapers, in that order. MBC radio's transmitter footprint covers almost the entire country. Wireless ownership is fairly extensive, with almost every village thought to have at least one set for group listening. Private radio is extending steadily from the main urban centres, but its reach into the rural areas is dependent on the growth in advertising revenue, commercial sponsorship of programmes and the willingness of the government to grant transmitter licences.

The spillover of these new urban transmitters does allow for listening in rural areas within 30 kilometres or so radius. However, for a large majority of voters, MBC radio is the only source of information available to them. MBC radio has continued to give totally unlimited access to the incumbent party. This has produced a lack of balance in the amount of time given to news of the rallies, meetings, the manifestos, policies and personalities of the contesting parties and independent candidates.

On MBC radio, very little time was given in the main news bulletins to parties other than the ruling alliance of UDF/AFORD/NCD. Often during the campaign period, several days passed without any mention in the main news bulletins of the campaigns of opposition candidates or parties. Both MBC radio and TVM chose to restrict their extended coverage of election rallies to those of the ruling alliance's presidential candidate, Bingu wa Mutharika, almost all of which were dominated by the head of state, outgoing President Bakili Muluzi. The justification claimed for this monopoly of rally coverage is said to be the right of the head of state to have all his or her activities covered live by the media.

The degree of the imbalance was so large that the Commonwealth Media Adviser to the Malawi Electoral Commission (MEC) reported (from a detailed monitoring operation he had been supervising for the Commission since the beginning of the year) that over 90 per cent of all election coverage on MBC radio during the eight-week official campaign period had been about and of positive benefit to the ruling alliance (UDF/AFORD/NCD). The figure for TVM had been just over 80 per cent. In the final few days of campaigning, our observers saw a small measure of improvement in TVM's balance, but this was too late to be any remedy for the grossly undemocratic coverage throughout the official campaign period and before.

Of the private radio services, which are now having an impact and providing an alternative voice for the voters, Capital Radio (FM 102.5) – which broadcasts news bulletins every half hour – has provided the most balanced election coverage since the start of campaigning on 20 March.

The MEC Media Monitoring Unit noted that Capital Radio gave 24 per cent of its campaign coverage to the UDF/AFORD/NCD coalition; 24 per cent to the Mgwirizano Coalition; 20 per cent to the National Democratic Alliance (NDA); 15 per cent to independent candidate Justin Malewezi; 10 per cent to the Malawi Congress Party (MCP); and 7 per cent to others.

The Malawi Institute of Journalism (MIJ) radio (FM 90.3) and Power 101 FM, while giving substantial positive coverage to all the main parties, showed bias against the ruling UDF/AFORD/NCD alliance and its presidential candidate by the much larger amount of negative news broadcast about them compared with that given to opposition parties.

Television

TVM said it would work closely with the Electoral Commission and all the contesting political parties to provide coverage in the run-up to the Presidential and Parliamentary elections. However, 80 per cent of its election coverage was focused on the ruling alliance. TVM was one of the signatories to the Malawi National Peace Commitment, an initiative of the government-backed Forum for Dialogue and Peace that promoted dialogue, peace-building and non-violent conflict resolution within Malawian society. One of the principles of Chapter Six of the Commitment states that the media will commit itself: 'To provide all political parties equitable access to our media houses'.

TVM said that there was a lack of equipment and resources to provide equitable coverage of all political parties during the campaign period. They argued that election coverage required additional resources such as transport, tapes, cameras and editing equipment, but that the station had not received any additional budget or equipment to support them. TVM was also unable to cover some political rallies as some parties had barred them from covering their events.

Guidelines, monitoring and action

Both MBC radio and TVM television have ignored key elements in the media guidelines and the requirements of the Parliamentary and Presidential Elections Act of 1993, the Local Government Elections Act of 1996, and the Communications Act of 1998, which all call for full, fair and balanced political coverage at all times in news and other broadcasts related to campaigns of all registered candidates and parties during the campaign period. These guidelines are intended to require that the media provide the public with civic education and information about the electoral process and the rights of each citizen to cast his/her ballot. Voter education is a crucial building block of democracy, and in this election, voter education and balanced information were inadequate.

At the request of the Electoral Commission, a media adviser was provided by the Commonwealth Secretariat for a series of visits from mid-2002 to May 2004. The adviser, Tim Neale, helped the Commission, the political parties and the news organisations to redraft the guidelines for media coverage of the elections. From January 2004 he was also tasked with establishing and supervising a media monitoring operation to allow the Commission to acquire detailed information about the relative balance being provided throughout the campaign by radio, television and the press. In the run-up to the elections, the Commonwealth Secretariat made clear that it was disturbed by the bias of the state media.

The Electoral Commission and the Malawi Communications Regulatory Authority (MACRA) failed to ensure that the media abided by the law by providing equal coverage to the political parties and their candidates during the campaign. The ruling UDF/AFORD/NCD coalition had a distinct advantage in the election campaign, with MBC radio and TVM at its disposal. Almost all of the ruling party's campaign rallies were covered in the news and in extended broadcasts often amounting to 20 hours per week. There was no distinction made between coverage of the head of state in the performance of his duties and his campaign advocacy for his UDF presidential candidate, Bingu wa Mutharika. There was a clear bias towards the ruling party led by President Muluzi and his chosen successor. Over 90 per cent of election coverage on MBC radio was given to the UDF/AFORD/NCD party.

The Electoral Commission acknowledged in a newspaper advertisement in the Weekend Nation (15–16 May 2004) that 'election coverage by MBC has been weighted in favour of the current government. This is unacceptable and poses a threat to democracy'. The Commission said it had 'requested the balance be redressed', but the pro-ruling party bias continued until the eve of polling day. MBC radio and TVM had agreed in writing to abide by the Electoral Commission's media guidelines on electoral coverage, but failed to do so.

Party broadcasts

Recordings of party manifestos that the Electoral Commission had sent to MBC radio on 3 May for broadcast were not aired. This contravenes Part V Section 63 (2) and Part V Section 63 (1) (b) of the Parliamentary and Presidential Elections Act (1993), which called for neutrality and balance. MBC radio said some political party broadcasts could not be aired due to the low quality of the programmes subcontracted to private production houses by the MEC, which was 'the substandard nature of some of the recordings'. MBC radio also cited 'the lack of commitment from some of the parties to record with MBC and the non-availability of opposition politicians for interviews'. Despite the setbacks faced by MBC radio, its spokesman said the station was determined to 'send out reporters to all the districts for unofficial results announcement'.

The print media

Several newspapers emerged during the pre-election period. While some ran strongly partisan stories and comment, most avoided the worst excesses of personal abuse directed at individual candidates.

The main permanent daily papers (*The Nation* and *Daily Times*) took, overall, a line against the ruling alliance (UDF/AFORD/NCD). Nevertheless, they still gave substantial coverage to the manifestos of all the main parties and coalitions. Readers of either paper would therefore, over the period of the campaign, have had the chance to absorb the main thrust of all the policies being proposed by all contenders.

So far as the weekly newspapers were concerned, *The Chronicle*, a weekly newspaper, was strongly against the ruling alliance and favoured the opposition. *The Enquirer* featured positive headlines and stories on the ruling UDF/AFORD/NCD coalition and negative stories on the opposition, portraying them as being in disarray, lacking co-operation and unity, with no manifestos and vision for the leadership of the country. The *Saturday Post* and *Malawi Standard* are pro-ruling alliance newspapers. *The Exclusive*, a pro-ruling coalition paper which emerged only early this year, was blatantly against the opposition, branding the candidates as liars and incompetent to govern the country.

Voter education

Both MBC radio and TVM performed poorly in providing voter education. MBC radio acknowledged that the station's role included civic education and information. Its representatives had met Electoral Commission officials in March 2003 to discuss voter education programmes and this led to the establishment of an MBC radio task force on elections. But MBC said it faced many constraints in producing programmes: it said that these included a lack of transport and allowances from the Electoral Commission for MBC radio reporters.

We [the observer group] noted that the NGO Gender Coordination Network co-operated with MBC radio to profile female parliamentary candidates in their campaign programmes.

TVM said it was not accredited as a civic education provider for the elections, but was open to co-operation with accredited NGOs responsible for civic education. It had worked with the National Democratic Institute and GTZ in running some political debates.

The print media did a better job in voter education compared to the electronic media. *The Nation*, *Daily Times* and *The Chronicle* featured articles on the candidates, with editorial comments and analysis of various political parties and the impact on the political landscape of the country if respective parties or candidates were voted into power.

The Nation ran a seven-page supplement on several occasions produced by the NGO Gender Coordination Network. This profiled female parliamentary candidates and highlighted the Southern Africa Development Community (SADC) objective that 30 per cent of parliamentarians in each member country should be female.

Commonwealth Observer Group report

Seychelles Election, 2006

Note: *The 2006 Presidential Election was contested by Mr James Michel (Seychelles People's Progressive Party [SPPF]); Mr Wavel Ramkalawan (SNP); and Mr Philippe Boullé (Independent).*

Media

Seychelles does not have a large and diverse media industry; this is perpetuated by the prohibitive cost of establishing and operating a private television or radio station. The country is served mainly by the Seychelles Broadcasting Corporation (SBC), a state-owned public broadcaster that runs one television channel and one radio station. In addition to SBC, there is one daily newspaper, *The Seychelles Nation*, which is a government-owned newspaper whose mandate is to report government news and business.

Three weekly party newspapers exist: *The People* (SPPF), *Regar* (SNP) and *Seychelles Weekly* (DP). We heard that another newspaper, *The Independent*, resumed publication prior to the elections. The team did not, however, meet with the editor.

Given that there is no independent media in Seychelles, the role of SBC as the public broadcaster is of great importance. As a public broadcaster, the SBC should provide news and information in an impartial and balanced fashion.

The team commends SBC and the Electoral Commissioner for facilitating an agreement with the political parties which ensured all presidential candidates (and their parties) received equal opportunity to use SBC (television and radio) for party political broadcasts and spots (PPBs) to promote their agendas.

The team was able to see and hear some of the PPBs towards the end of the campaign, and see some of the news coverage relating to the campaign. There were allegations by political parties of unfair treatment in respect of coverage of their events and prejudicial portrayal of their views.

5 Guiding Principles

Having discussed the critical issues for the media in covering an election, we now turn to the guiding principles for the media in election mode.

Protection of Sources

Protection of sources is about building and maintaining trust with one's sources. It involves a journalist being able to protect the identity of his or her informants, and being prepared to resist pressure or persecution to reveal how he or she has obtained news. Protection of sources is one of the hallmarks of being a journalist.

Accountability and Truth

Against this background, journalists should strive to achieve credibility in their reporting, to the extent that they would like to be identified with their report. Twentieth-century American writer and journalist, Walter Lipman, in his seminal book *Public Opinion* (1922), argued that the function of news is to signal an event, not to provide a true picture of reality upon which readers could act. Edward J Epstein (1966), another American journalist, further suggests that we might all be better served if reporters admitted that, because of inescapable limitations, they are merely circulators of partial information, and not establishers of truth. Clearly, handling questions of ethics that arise in their work remains a matter of personal integrity for individual reporters, with or without recourse to a written code.

Most of the ethical and professional issues that journalists encounter in covering elections are variants of those they confront everyday in their working lives. However, some election-coverage issues and dilemmas may present themselves in particular ways. Examples of professional dilemmas include: newsworthiness versus balanced coverage, transparency versus integrity of the election process and reporting inflammatory speech (see below and accompanying examples).

Newsworthiness v. balanced coverage

News coverage is typically driven by considerations of what is distinct and of particular interest in any event. Yet voters require a fair and balanced presentation of manifestos and agenda of different parties, which may not necessarily be distinct or interesting. How can the media reconcile its news function with this public service function? The answer, according to journalist Ibrahim Helal, an Egyptian working for Al Jazeera, is simple: 'We are trying our best to be comprehensive and accurate. To be accurate, not to achieve an ideological aim'.[36] See, for example, the text box opposite written by *Washington Post* Ombudsman Deborah Howell.

In the example opposite, while the *Washington Post* has printed more stories on Senator Obama than on Senator McCain, the *Washington Post* ombudsman considers here whether the argument of newsworthiness justifies the imbalance. Each editor will need to reach his or her own conclusion about these two competing priorities, just as staff members of the *Washington Post* have done. In the end, the US journalists working alongside Deborah Howell justify their decision on the basis of their professional judgement of newsworthiness. They make a solid and convincing argument.

Transparency versus integrity of the election process

One of the reasons that the media plays an essential role in democratic elections is that it is able to subject the election

---

Box 5.1 Fraudster selected to contest elections

Fraudster Omutela Abekhuya has been nominated to contest the general election unopposed on the Ematetie Peoples Party (EPP) ticket. This is the same Mr Abekhuya, who only a few months ago was found guilty by the High Court of failing to pay his income tax and for not remitting the pension deductions of his staff to the National Pensions Agency. Mr Abekhuya is not in prison only because he reached an out-of-court settlement to pay all that he owed.

---

process to scrutiny and to expose any malpractice. However, proper administration of an election also depends on security and confidentiality. Balancing these two elements is an issue for lawmakers and those responsible for drawing up electoral regulations. However, it is also a day-to-day practical issue for journalists themselves. See, for example, the text box entitled 'Fraudster selected to contest elections'.

In our view, this story does not measure up to the journalist

Box 5.2 Obama's edge in the coverage race

By Deborah Howell
Washington Post, Sunday, 17 August 2008, page B06

Democrat Barack Obama has had about a 3 to 1 advantage over Republican John McCain in *Post* page 1 stories since Obama became his party's presumptive nominee June 4. Obama has generated a lot of news by being the first African American nominee, and he is less well known than McCain – and therefore there's more to report on. But the disparity is so wide that it doesn't look good.

In overall political stories from June 4 to Friday, Obama dominated by 142 to 96. Obama has been featured in 35 stories on page 1; McCain has been featured in 13, with three page 1 references with photos to stories on inside pages. Fifteen stories featured both candidates and were about polls or issues such as terrorism, social security and the candidates' agreement on what should be done in Afghanistan.

This dovetails with Obama's dominance in photos, which I pointed out two weeks ago. At that time, it was 122 for Obama and 78 for McCain. Two weeks later, it's 143 to 100, almost the same gap, because editors have run almost the same number of photos – 21 of Obama and 22 of McCain – since they realized the disparity. McCain is almost even with Obama in page 1 photos – 10 to 9.

This is not just a *Post* phenomenon. The Project for Excellence in Journalism has been monitoring campaign coverage at an assortment of large and medium-circulation newspapers, broadcast evening and morning news shows, five news websites, three major cable news networks, and public radio and other radio outlets. Its latest report, for the week of Aug. 4–10, shows that for the eighth time in nine weeks, Obama received significantly more coverage than McCain.

Obama's dominance on page 1 is partly due to stories about his winning the bruising primary battle with Hillary Rodham Clinton and his trip overseas in July. The coverage of June 4, 5, 6 and 7 led to six page 1 stories in *The Post*, including Obama's nomination victory, his strategy, elation among African Americans over the historic nature of his win and his fundraising advantage. Then he made an appearance at Nissan Pavilion with Virginia's Gov. Timothy Kaine and Sen. James Webb, and it became a local page 1 story. During those few days, there was one page 1 reference to an inside-page story about McCain going after Clinton's disgruntled supporters.

When Obama traveled to the Middle East and Europe, the coverage dwarfed that of McCain – six page 1 stories from July 19 to July 27, plus an earlier front-page story announcing the trip. McCain managed one page 1 story and one page 1 reference; the July 25 story said he might pick a vice presidential candidate soon, but that didn't happen. While there was no front-page story about Obama on July 25, it seemed wrong not to count that day because a photo of him in Berlin dominated the front page. I also counted a story about a *Post*-ABC News poll concerning racism and its potential impact on the election; 3 in 10 of those polled acknowledged racial bias.

Not all page 1 coverage has been favorable. Obama was hit right away with two page 1 stories about Washington insider James A Johnson, a former Fannie Mae CEO, who was criticized for mortgage deals and then withdrew from vetting Obama's potential running mates. A story about Obama's former Chicago church reminded readers of the controversy over his former pastor, the Rev. Jeremiah Wright Jr. There were also stories with a favorable cast – about his patriotism, his first appearance with Clinton and the coverage from his foreign trip.

McCain's page 1 stories were a mix – a story about the flap over former senator Phil Gramm's comment about a 'nation of whiners' over the economy and a story about conservatives wanting to battle McCain on the party platform. But there also were stories about plans to make the federal government more environmentally responsible and McCain's proposal for offshore drilling.

The single most revealing story about McCain – and one of the best *Post* stories on either candidate – was a top-of-the-front-page look at McCain's intellect. The story, by veteran reporter and editor Robert G. Kaiser, was the kind of analysis that tells readers something they didn't know. It was neither positive nor negative, just revealing and insightful.

Another favorite was by business reporter Lori Montgomery on how both candidates will have trouble lowering the deficit with their spending plans. A change of pace was movie critic Stephen Hunter's look at McCain and Obama as film icons – McCain as John Wayne and Obama as Will Smith.

Page 1 coverage isn't all that counts, but it is the most visible. Certainly there were many stories on the politics page and elsewhere in the paper. (I'm not counting opinion columns.) The Trail, *The Post's* politics blog, had dozens of short items about both candidates, all interesting to political junkies. Post inside coverage has been a mix of horse-race coverage – stories about endorsements, advisers, who can win where – and issues stories.

Style stories have dealt with the Internet, voters and volunteers, and the cultural aspects of the campaigns. Cindy McCain was featured in a big style spread and Michelle Obama in a metro story about her recent visit to Virginia.

Numbers aren't everything in political coverage, but readers deserve comparable coverage of the candidates.

Bill Hamilton, assistant managing editor for politics, thinks that I'm wrong to put weight on numbers. 'We make our own decisions about what we consider newsworthy. We are not garment workers measuring our product every day to fulfill somebody's quota. That means as editors we decide what we think is important, because that's what our readers look for us to do – not to adhere to some arbitrary standard.

'The nomination of the first African American presidential nominee after a bitter primary campaign and his efforts to unite a party afterward were simply more newsworthy than a candidate whose nomination was already assured and who spent much of that time raising money. In the end, we can and should be judged on the fairness of our coverage, but that is a judgment that must be made over the course of the whole campaign, not a single period of time'.

principles of maintaining balance and impartiality. Indeed, it raises questions about the decision-making processes of this newsroom. It puts labels and opinion into a news story and makes a judgement, instead of presenting both sides of the story and allowing readers or listeners to judge. The editor has to decide whether the story, and in this particular case the language and tone, are in the public interest and offer the right balance between the competing subjects of transparency versus integrity of the election process.

Reporting inflammatory speech

A paradox is that election campaigns are the times when politicians are most likely to express extreme and inflammatory sentiments – with the chance of such views reaching large audiences. Added to this, elections are the time when extreme views are most likely to have a negative impact, at the same time that campaigning is when expression of differing political views is most important. The regulatory implications of this complex dilemma are for policy-makers to resolve. For journalists, the challenge is to report inflammatory political speech in a manner that is both accurate and least likely to provoke violence or fear. See, for example, the text box entitled 'Kenya Poll Violence: Spreading the Word of Hate'.

Box 5.3 Kenya poll violence: spreading the word of hate

NAIROBI, 22 January 2008, Integrated Regional Information Networks (IRIN)

Inflammatory statements and songs broadcast on vernacular radio stations and at party rallies, text messages, emails, posters and leaflets have all contributed to post-electoral violence in Kenya, according to analysts. Hundreds of homes have been burnt, more than 600 people killed and 250,000 displaced.

While the mainstream media, both English and Swahili, have been praised for their even-handedness, vernacular radio broadcasts have been of particular concern, given the role of Kigali's Radio-Télévision Libre des Mille Collines in inciting people to slaughter their neighbours in the Rwandan genocide of 1994.

'There's been a lot of hate speech, sometimes thinly veiled. The vernacular radio stations have perfected the art', Caesar Handa, Chief Executive of Strategic Research, told IRIN, 'The call-in shows are the most notorious', said Handa. 'The announcers don't really have the ability to check what the callers are going to say'.

Source: UN News Agency IRIN published on 22 January 2008. See: *http://www.irinnews.org/* [accessed 12 January 2009]

UN news agency, IRIN, does well to explain the dilemma and issues in the above example. The agency[37] notes that one difficulty in monitoring vernacular (local language/community) radio statios is that the language used is often quite subtle and obscure. In Rwanda, for example, the term 'cockroaches' was used in reference to genocide targets, while in Kenya, various community stations with ethnic audiences called other tribes 'mongooses who have stolen our chicken', i.e. 'thieves who have stolen our land'. The end result is that other communities are dehumanised in the eyes (or ears) and minds of the station's listeners, who then assault communities they now perceive to be their enemies without a sense of any guilt.

IRIN quote Caesar Handa, Chief Executive of private polling company Strategic Research, as saying, 'Hate speech is contributing in a big way to get people to take action as a result of the anger they have been feeling individually. You might have an individual feeling, but when entire communities are rallied to a cause, people find justification and find the community would support them …'.

Again, it is for editors to choose between whether to air a broadcast or not, taking into consideration any knowledge they have that the broadcast could, for example, seriously damage the electoral environment and render credible elections impossible.

Codes of Ethics or Conduct

Journalism is often described as a 'profession' and many journalists are proud to be considered professionals. Other journalists regard their job or career to be a 'trade', rather than a profession such as medicine or law. Whatever the conclusion, there is broad agreement that the practice of journalism needs to be regulated by a professional standard or ethical code. A reporter's credibility and reputation are judged to be alive and well only if his or her last story was in line with such a code of accepted standards.

Codes of conduct may be promulgated by associations or trade unions of journalists, by media houses, individually or collectively, or by regulatory bodies. Such codes are most effective if they are the outcome of a collective process in which journalists and editors themselves participate. There are overarching principles, as ratified by the International Federation of Journalists.[38]

Codes generally underpin news values and ethics relevant to journalists covering elections. News values include, for example, accuracy, impartiality, honesty and resistance to corruption, avoiding use of language or sentiments that promote violence or discrimination, and correction of inaccurate factual reporting. However, it is often good practice for every newsroom to also develop a code of conduct that covers issues that are specific to elections. Such a code will work better if it is agreed by the national union of journalists in the country concerned, or even one that is embraced across the region. Election-specific issues include reporting opinion poll findings, reporting political rallies and other campaign events, using exit polls and reporting the vote count.

We are aware that many countries have general codes of conduct to guide or regulate journalists in their work. For example, the global news and information company Thomson Reuters has codes of conduct that all its journalists sign up to as part of their contract. All Thomson Reuters journalists are judged on the basis of that code, and there are consequences for any breaches, including instant dismissal from duty. Bloomberg News, another global financial news service, notes that is has adopted a code of ethics to maintain its professional reputation, to ensure accurate and unbiased news reporting and to protect itself and its employees against accusations of partiality in reporting news. 'As such, *violations of this standard of conduct can result in suspension or dismissal*'.[39]

The general principles contained in these ethical codes form the basis for the professional standards that journalists and editors should uphold at all times, including during election periods. Yet, as discussed above, it is also useful to develop a specific code of conduct to address the particular professional dilemmas that may arise during elections in greater detail.

Media codes of conduct are most effective when practitioners themselves are involved in drawing them up. The standards in the code are then seen as aids to effective journalism and not restrictions. Some codes are drawn up by media practitioners alone, while others involve consultation with other stakeholders, including the electoral management body and political parties.

Elements of a code of conduct

A code of conduct for election reporting should ideally include a mixture of general ethical standards, applicable in all circumstances, and those specific to election periods. The United Nations Educational, Scientific and Cultural Organization (UNESCO), as well as regional media organisations across the world, have carried out a certain amount of work in this regard. Below is a suggested check-list of standards, derived from the International Institute for Democracy and Electoral Assistance (International IDEA)'s proposed code of conduct, itself based upon many existing codes from different countries[40] and aimed at the journalist as a professional:

- The first duty of a journalist is to report accurately and without bias.

- A journalist shall report only in accordance with facts of which s/he knows the origin. A journalist shall not suppress essential information.

- A journalist shall observe professional secrecy regarding the source of information obtained in confidence.

- A journalist shall report in a balanced manner. If a candidate makes an allegation against another candidate, the journalist should seek comment from both sides wherever possible.

- A journalist shall do the utmost to correct any published information that is found to be harmfully inaccurate.

- As far as possible, a journalist shall report the views of candidates and political parties directly and in their own words, rather than as they are described by others.

- A journalist shall avoid using language or expressing sentiments that may further discrimination or violence on any grounds, including race, sex, sexual orientation, language, religion, political or other opinions, and national or social origins.

- When reporting the opinions of those who do advocate discrimination or violence, a journalist shall do the utmost to put such views in a clear context and to report the opinions of those against whom such sentiments are directed.

- A journalist shall not accept any inducement from a politician or candidate.

- A journalist shall not make any promise to a politician about the content of a news report.

- A journalist shall take care in reporting the findings of opinion polls. Any report should, wherever possible, include the following information:
  - who commissioned and carried out the poll and when,
  - the number of people interviewed, where and how were they interviewed and the margin of error, and
  - what was the exact wording of the questions.

- A journalist shall regard the following as grave professional offences:
  - plagiarism,
  - malicious misrepresentation,
  - calumny, slander, libel or unfounded accusations, and
  - acceptance of a bribe in any form in consideration of either publication or suppression.

Codes for media houses, political parties and electoral bodies

We have now looked at codes governing the ethics, conduct and even behaviour of journalists in dealing with various stake-holders when they are covering elections. We, the authors, now suggest a code of conduct for media houses and others, based on the work of other media organisations in this area.[41] This code covers four broad areas, encompassing different obligations attached to the three groups of stakeholders. Some issues, such as the question of what system is adopted for direct access by political parties and the media, are not directly addressed in this code. Such issues are likely to be addressed by national laws, regulations or agreements between stakeholders. Likewise, the question of how the provisions in such a code could be enforced depends upon extraneous factors.

Media houses

- In all media, there shall be a clear separation between fact and comment. News reporting should reflect the facts as they are honestly perceived by journalists. Comment may reflect the editorial line of the publication.

- Publicly owned media shall not express an editorial opinion in favour of or against any party or candidate.

- Publicly owned media have a duty to be balanced and impartial in their election reporting and not to discriminate against any party in granting access to airtime.

- If media houses accept paid political advertising, they shall do so on a non-discriminatory basis and at equal rates for all parties.

- News, interviews, information or current affairs programmes or articles in the public media shall not be biased in favour of or against any party or candidate.

- The media shall provide equitable and regular coverage to all political parties, their candidates and platforms.

- The media shall encourage and provide access to voters to express their opinions and views.

- The media shall promote democratic values such as the rule of good law, accountability and good governance.

- Any candidate or party that makes a reasonable claim of having been defamed or otherwise injured by a broadcast or publication shall either be granted the opportunity to reply or be entitled to a correction or retraction by the broadcaster or publisher or by the person who made the allegedly defamatory statement. The reply or correction shall be broadcast or published as soon as possible.

- News coverage of press conferences and public statements concerning matters of political controversy (as opposed to functions of state) called or made by the head of government, government ministers, or members of parliament shall be subject to a right of reply or equal time rules. This obligation acquires even greater force when the person making the statement is also standing for office.

- Publicly owned media shall publish or broadcast voter education material.

- Voter education material shall be accurate and impartial and must effectively inform voters about the voting process, including: how, when and where to vote, to register to vote and to verify proper registration; the secrecy of the ballot (and thus safety from retaliation); the importance of voting; the functions of the offices that are under contention; and similar matters.

- Voter education shall include programmes in minority languages and programmes targeted for groups that traditionally may have been excluded from the political process, such as women and people with disabilities.

- Media houses should monitor their own output to make sure that it conforms to the standards set out in this code of conduct.

The media does indeed take these standards seriously. For example, in November 2008 (ahead of general elections in April 2009), public broadcaster the South African Broadcasting Corporation (SABC) held meetings with the regulator (the Independent Communications Authority of South Africa [ICASA]), the Independent Elections Commission (IEC) and political parties and committed to the following standard:

- To adhere to the legislative and regulatory framework established to ensure free and fair coverage and to ensure that the editorial code and policies are followed.

- News decisions during elections, as it is always done, will be driven by judgement of news staff and that they will take into account the views, policies and campaigns of all political parties. Editors will make decisions on news value and not political agendas.

- That any pressures and complains experienced by our editorial staff – where political parties seek to influence editorial decision – should be reported to the relevant editorial and regulatory heads.

- All news and programming staff are required to familiarise themselves with the ICASA election guidelines as well as the SABC's editorial policies and the guidelines developed for election coverage. They must also ensure that they are rigorously followed and implemented.

- In addition to its usual coverage and programmes, the SABC also committed to go an extra mile in its election coverage and gathering of material for special election programmes by:

  – utilising its networks of journalists to gather material from rural and urban areas of the country, to tell the stories of citizens in the villages and cities, and the stories of politicians, parties and their campaigns,

  – using its bureaus all over the world to provide foreign perspectives on the elections, and

  – utilising its broadcast facilities to take programmes to the people and election events, and to tell the stories from where the people are, in as many languages as possible within platform limitations.

  – providing platforms for citizens, as well as politicians and political parties, to relay their campaign messages on national, regional and provincial programming on an equitable basis as prescribed in the ICASA election regulations.

  – offering wide and balanced analysis of election issues by a panel of election analysts on its platforms.

  – providing results broadcasts as and when the IEC releases them in a way that will inform, contextualise and explain them to our audiences and viewers.[42]

Political parties

We have established the importance of codes of conduct and now turn to another difficult and complex issue – the conduct of political parties in dealing with journalists. A growing number of countries have adopted codes of conduct governing the behaviour of political parties and candidates during elections, while the conduct of electoral officials is also subject to strict professional standards. We see overlaps in these three sets of ethical standards.

The media is increasingly recognised as playing a crucial role in free and democratic elections, particularly by communicating political messages from parties and candidates, by relaying important voter information from election administrators, and by subjecting the election process to independent scrutiny and comment.

The crucial role of the mass media imposes particular ethical obligations on journalists and editors, in the same way that other codes present an obligation to other stakeholders. There have been suggestions that a joint code of conduct be adopted by all stakeholders – the mass media, political parties and electoral authorities – to ensure that they behave ethically and respect one another's rights and freedoms. Below are outline guidelines for a code regarding the conduct of political parties in dealing with the media:

- All political parties and candidates shall respect the freedom of the media.

- Political parties and candidates shall not harass or obstruct journalists who are engaged in their professional activities.

- Incumbent political parties and candidates shall not abuse their office to gain unfair advantage in access to the media. This provision applies to all media, but is of particular relevance when publicly funded media are under direct control by the government of the day.

- Political parties and candidates shall not offer bribes or inducements to journalists or media houses to encourage them to attend campaign events or to report favourably on the party or unfavourably on other parties or candidates.

- Political parties and candidates should not misrepresent the stated positions or any other factual information about other parties and candidates.

- Political parties and candidates should avoid using language that is inflammatory or defamatory, or that threatens or incites violence against any other person or group.

- The party leaderships shall ensure that the standards of tolerance and free debate contained in this code of conduct are communicated and fully explained to campaign workers. Parties should take full responsibility for the words and actions of those campaigning on their behalf.

Electoral management bodies

The Electoral Commission, as the body that manages political transition, is the most important institution in any democracy. It is necessary that an Electoral Commission have absolute integrity and is respected by all players: political parties, civil society and other citizens. Where such a body has failed to live up to its tasks and obligations, as in Kenya in 2007 and Zimbabwe in 2008, conflict – often violent – has followed. That is why an Election Commission's relationship with media deserves scrutiny. We share guidelines on what should shape this relationship below:

- Electoral management bodies shall respect the freedom of the media, including their editorial independence and right to express political preferences.

- Electoral management bodies shall respect the right to freedom of expression of parties and candidates.

- Electoral management bodies shall conduct the election in an open and transparent manner.

- Electoral management bodies shall endeavour to make sure that their activities are open to scrutiny by the media to the fullest extent possible.

- Electoral management bodies should not favour any media outlet in the distribution of either paid advertising or free information material.

- Electoral management bodies should use the mass media, among other means, to convey timely and accurate information to enable the electorate to exercise their right to vote in an informed manner.

- Electoral management bodies should only impose such restrictions on reporting – for example, at the polling station and the count – as are strictly necessary to ensure the integrity of the electoral process.

TESTIMONY

Milton Walker – Jamaica

My first experience in covering a national election was in 1993 when I reported for the state-run Jamaica Broadcasting Corporation (JBC). It was a tense period, as the newsroom was divided with some reporters supporting the opposition party and others subservient to the ruling party. The director of TV news was appointed by the ruling party and in fact was known to have been a supporter of that party.

The tradition had been for the station to be essentially a mouthpiece for the government and established interests in Jamaica. The opposition was rarely given a significant voice in the state-owned media. There was frequent interference from the director, as he sought to push the party line. This led to frequent clashes. I remember one morning the director called the producer of the morning news bulletin after the 7a.m. newscast and demanded to know why she had led with a story from the opposition leader. There were also calls from government ministers to the newsroom, upset with particular stories and demanding more favourable coverage. The atmosphere was highly charged around election times, as the station would be attacked verbally. Opposition supporters would hurl verbal abuse at the crews covering political assignments, although none was ever harmed physically. Soldiers were always deployed on the compound a couple weeks before an election, leaving a few days after the poll.

Covering the actual election was a challenging task in and of itself. Jamaica is a mountainous island with several mountain ranges running across the island. This makes television transmission a nightmare. On Election Day, the engineers would perform miracles so we could get footage back from various cities, towns and regions all over the island. We were able to send back video and audio broadcasts from three locations outside the capital. This was very exciting and rewarding, as on a normal day we would have to drive back into the television studios in the capital to show the footage on air. I was sent to cover the south-western and central region of the island, with the highlight being responsible for covering the Prime Minister voting in his constituency. In the evening, I was assigned to a counting centre to observe the vote-counting process and send back results for that station. The elections of 1993 were also unique, as this was the first time we used cellular telephones to communicate with the station and colleagues. This allowed us to respond to events quickly as we were constantly in touch.

'The elections of 1993 were also very unique as this was the first time we used cellular telephones to communicate with the station and colleagues. This allowed us to respond to events quickly as we were constantly in touch.'

Milton Walker

Shortly after the 1993 elections, I moved to the privately run CVM Television station as news editor. This was a new era for media in Jamaica, as it was the first time big business had owned a major national electronic outlet with a potentially powerful voice. How would it deal with editorial matters? Would it pander to its own narrow sector interests? Suffice it to say, most of those fears were not realised (at least in the first seven years), as the owners took an almost hands-off approach. The newsroom was also helped by the fact that there were early divisions on the board and ownership, which probably distracted any thoughts of interference. We also had a team that strongly upheld journalistic conventions.

We quickly set about crafting an editorial policy that would be the framework for an independent news agenda. It included all the desirable features – fairness, objectivity, right of reply, equal time for the opposition – which any well-run newsroom had. We also decided to broaden the range of issues we covered to include matters previously untouched.

Among these issues were rural news, inner city matters, corruption in the public service, crime and police excess. But it's in the coverage of political matters that I believe we made the most valuable contribution to the deepening of our democracy. For the first time, the opposition and civil society had a reasonable opportunity to voice its concern about government policy and put forward alternative views on television, the most powerful medium in Jamaica (the election of 3 September 2008 was largely believed to have been won on TV).

During parliamentary debates, we carried all speakers, including the opposition ones, live and gave equal time to all. We were also free to criticise all parties without fear of retribution or sanction. On the campaign trail, we gave both parties equal coverage: if we covered one rally live, we gave the same amount of time to the other. We also gave both parties a set number of minutes of airtime for free, often in prime time. Additionally, a political party was free to pay for airtime whenever they wished.

However, there is another side to covering elections in Jamaica. Elections are generally exciting periods with motorcades, rallies, biting political ads on television and a usually festive atmosphere, although there are incidents of violence in some areas. In one year, a strong third party emerged on the scene and contested all 60 seats in the parliament. Because opinion polls suggested it could win several seats, the media decided to offer the party equal time and provided roughly the same level of coverage as the other two main parties received. This posed quite a challenge, as with our meagre resources we are often unable to cover every single event. We do get assistance from some independent television companies, and sometimes the political parties record their rallies themselves. However, we accept tapes from the parties only if they provide the unedited copy of, say, the leaders' speeches.

Marshalling all the footage and material from all over the country can be quite a challenge. In earlier times, we used couriers and Jamaica's domestic airline to fly our tapes back to the capital, where we could broadcast the material. Needless to say, this was a risky undertaking, although loss of a tape was extremely rare. On Election Day, we often devoted all our resources to coverage of each administrative region's key seats, in particular the marginal seats that often decide who wins the poll. There are also the national debates to consider, which are organised by the Debates Commission and manned by the Media and Press Associations. There are usually three debates involving the leaders, the finance spokespeople and a third sector area decided on the basis of issues.

There is also a downside to covering elections in Jamaica. The battle for political power can be fierce and intense, and some supporters get carried away. There is also violence in some inner-city and low-income areas located in marginal seats. These issues are tough and sometimes risky to cover. Journalists have been threatened and shot at – though thankfully none has ever been injured. On the night of the general election in 2002, shots were fired in the vicinity of our station (we heard them from inside the building). Our general manager's car was shot at while she drove home on election night. We don't believe she was targeted, but it was a frightening experience. There are other challenges as well: during the elections of 2002, our cameraman and news editor were detained and their camera seized by the police during an incident at a polling station in the central region. They were later released after we complained to the Ministry of National Security and the Police Commissioner.[43]

Makereta Komai – Fiji Islands

A military coup in Fiji in December 2006 ousted the last democratically elected government – Laisenia Qarase – and ushered in an interim government, led by military strongman, Commodore Frank Bainimarama. On taking power, the Commodore told his island country as well as the international community that he was committed to returning Fiji to full democracy as soon as possible.

The head of the EU Delegation in the Pacific, Dr Roberto Ridolfi, has said that if Fiji delayed the conduct of polls for more than three years, funds allocated for sugar and other EU-funded projects would be further reduced – bringing economic pressure to bear on a political matter and an example of how foreign influence can affect the course of democracy. Fiji has agreed to a roadmap designed by the EU to take the country back to democracy and to have a general election during 2009.

Going back to the election of 2006, following a proclamation issued by the then Acting President, Ratu Joni Madraiwiwi, on 2 March 2006, parliament was dissolved on 27 March ahead of elections scheduled for 6–13 May. According to the then Supervisor of Elections, Semesa Karavaki, the extended voting period was due to an increase in the number of polling stations (1,096 compared to 796 in the previous elections).

Indigenous Fijians make up about 51 per cent of the country's approximately 880,000 population, while Indians make up 44 per cent. In the 71-member House of Representatives, 25 seats are open to all communities, while the remaining 46 are reserved for the country's different ethnic groups.

A total of 338 candidates, including 30 women, and 24 political parties registered for the elections. The elections were the third conducted under the 1997 Constitution, which brought about significant changes to the electoral process and the composition of the House of Representatives (parliament). They were held under a preferential voting system called the 'alternative vote', which is modelled on the Australian voting system. In the Pacific, Papua New Guinea and Nauru use the same voting system in a modified form. From independence in 1970, Fiji used the simple majority voting system or 'first past the post'. In the lead up to national elections, a nationwide registration of voters eligible to vote (those 21 years and over) was conducted to determine the electoral rolls.

Even though there was no national census, at the end of the voter registration it was confirmed that 480,000 voters would participate in the 2006 elections.

The main issue in the 2006 elections was the proposed Reconciliation Tolerance and Unity Bill, which included provisions for an amnesty for persons involved in the 2000 coup. The government argued that the slow pace of investigations and court hearings related to the coup represented an obstacle to its efforts to promote national unity. It insisted the bill would strengthen stability and peace by bringing the 'coup culture' to a close. However, the bill was severely criticised by the ethnic Indian community and academe. The Fiji Labour Party (FLP) and Fiji's military forces vowed to reject the bill. The highly politicised military slammed the bill as unfairly favouring indigenous Fijians. The final results gave a narrow majority to the ruling *Soqosoqo Duavata Ni Lewenivanua* (SDL) party, which won 36 of the 71 seats in the House of Representatives. Its rival, the FLP, took 31. The United Peoples Party (UPP) and independents took two seats each.[44]

TESTIMONY

Irene !Hoaes – Namibia

I covered the national and presidential elections for the Namibia Broadcasting Corporation (NBC) in 2004. I had been a journalist for a year. It was both a scary and an exciting experience. I did not know what to focus on, as the briefing was not really done properly. Voter turnout was much lower than the 80 per cent that voted in the first democratic elections in 1989, which catapulted the country's first black independence government to power.

In the intervening years, it appeared that apathy had set in, partly because political parties made promises along the way that they did not keep and people started changing their attitudes towards the whole concept of voting. For example, at independence there were promises of free education up to tertiary level, housing and opportunities for career building for every citizen. However, under the democratic rule the Government of Namibia chose after independence, all was not well, as many had anticipated. Education became unaffordable, especially for the low paid members of society, job opportunities were only for a few lucky ones, and to make matters worse, even those with academic training joined the thousands of unemployed on the streets. This situation led the electorate to change their minds: they now saw voting as enriching the chosen few or allowing politicians to go on enjoying their luxurious lifestyles without having to worry about the poor majority. One could also argue that voter apathy sets in because of lack of knowledge needed for informed participation, but counter arguments are that the political parties did not fulfil promises made during their election campaigns. One can also argue that few election campaigns have fully addressed key issues or the electorate's concerns.

I was assigned to cover or report on the election process in the three towns of Karibib, Omaruru and Usakos, and the surrounding rural areas, including communal and commercial farms located in the western part of the country (the Erongo Region). This is one of the regions where poor unemployed Namibians survive on less than one $1 a day, while a few make a living through small-scale mining or working as farm labourers on commercial farms. On the first day of the election, my duty started at Karibib Municipality, one of the town's two polling stations. The process was to start at seven o'clock, but by nine o'clock only five people had voted. My journey continued to Usakos, a neighbouring town located only 30 kilometres away. At the Usakos Municipality Hall, which is one of the town's three polling stations, I found about 100 people queuing and, according to the returning officer, more than 100 others had already cast their votes by midday (which was earlier that day).

My journey then continued to Omaruru, but I had to pass through Karibib Municipality and another polling station at a primary school, just to ascertain that the process was running smoothly. I was informed that only 300 voters had cast their ballots at both polling stations by midday, out of the 8,000 who had registered for the election. I went on to Omaruru, hoping that the situation in Usakos and Karibib would improve later in the day or during the second day of voting. At Omaruru, the situation was far better than in the other two towns. I observed that all three polling stations there recorded more than 1,000 voters each, bringing the total number of voters close to 4,000 or 48 per cent of those registered. Nonetheless, I observed generally that the Electoral Commission did not really create awareness, so people were unable to prepare themselves for the elections or did not even know when the election was on.

At some polling stations, there was no indication that an election was taking place. There was not even a single poster indicating that voting was due to take place at the villages. I personally think that more people would have voted, if only enough awareness had been created. This task was not only for the Electoral Commission, of course, but also includes the political parties, who should have created enough awareness to entice people to go and vote for them.

Another aspect that discourages people from voting are the long queues that they have to endure in the heat and sometimes rain before they can actually vote. With the country's new Electronic Voting System, hopefully things will improve, as this process is faster than the manual voting system.

Reporting on the actual voting process, the Namibia Broadcasting Corporation mostly focused on how many people voted, how many were turned away for not having the relevant documents at the time of voting, whether people were on time and how many could not vote by deadline. Other journalists focused on shortcomings, such as logistical problems, computers glitches or insufficient ballot papers or ballot papers that did not arrive in time.

For me, the main challenge was treading the fine line as a journalist for a state-run broadcaster – mindful of the unwritten mantra that we should not cast the government or its agencies in a bad light.[45]

Commonwealth Observer Group report

Uganda Election, 2006

Note: *Uganda was governed virtually as a no-party state and candidates had to contest as individuals in elections in the period after Yoweri Museveni came to power in 1986 after a five-year guerrilla war. But after 2001 domestic and international pressure for the restoration of multiparty democracy in Uganda became more persistent. In 2003 the Constitutional Court ruled that sections of the 2002 Political Parties and Organizations Act (PPOA) which prevented political parties from operating while the Movement system remained in place, were unconstitutional. The Court went further in 2004 to declare sections of the PPOA which restricted political meetings and the registration of political parties also unconstitutional. In July 2005, in accordance with the provisions of Article 69 of the Constitution, a second referendum was held to decide which political system to employ in the governance of the country. Despite the opposition boycotting the process and a low turn-out nationwide, the government supported the change and secured a 92% vote in favour of restoring multi-party elections. Parliament also voted controversially, in August 2005, to lift the constitutional two-term limit on the office of the President to allow unlimited terms. Several political parties emerged, or were revived, in expectation of the change to a multi-party dispensation. Parties such as the Uganda People's Congress (UPC), Democratic Party (DP) and Conservative Party (CP) which prior to 1986 had been permitted to exist, but not to contest elections under the Movement system, became fully operational. The National Resistance Movement-Organisation (NRM-O) became the political party created by the Movement system. New opposition groups also included the Reform Agenda (RA), now part of the Forum for Democratic Change (FDC), and cross-party pressure groups such as the Parliamentary Advocacy Forum (PAFO). There are other smaller political parties, but these do not make any significant electoral impact.*

Balance in news coverage

Members of the observer group listened to Ugandan radio stations, watched television news and election programmes, and read the English language national newspapers. During deployment, each two-person team was accompanied by a translator, who translated news programmes and newspapers produced in vernacular languages.

Our purpose was both to acquire information and to assess the balance of the media coverage of the elections. The group observed that both the state-owned *New Vision* and the privately owned *Daily Monitor* (the two daily newspapers with the largest circulations) made some efforts to provide a degree of balance in their coverage of the elections. Where treatment of a story in one paper displayed slant or bias, this was often counterbalanced by the treatment of the same story in the other. So coverage in the print media as a whole was somewhat balanced.

The electronic media were more demonstrably biased. The group observed, for example, that news coverage on UBC TV was overwhelmingly focused on the incumbent, with the other four candidates not receiving equitable treatment. The tone and portrayal of the incumbent's coverage also tended to be far more positive than that of other candidates. WBS TV was more balanced in its coverage of the two most prominent candidates, which nonetheless far exceeded that of the other three.

Media monitoring carried out by other international and domestic observer groups broadly confirmed our own assessment.[46] The European Union Election Observer Mission's data shows that the *New Vision* gave more positive and neutral coverage to the incumbent and more negative coverage to the Forum for Democratic Change (FDC) presidential candidate, than to any other candidate. The *Daily Monitor* gave more negative coverage to the incumbent than to any other candidate. Data provided by the Uganda Journalists Safety Committee (UJSC, part of the DEMGroup) shows that in the electronic media as a whole, coverage of the National Resistance Movement (NRM-O) tended to be more positive while that of the FDC was more neutral or negative.[47]

Regulation and laws

The principal legal provisions regarding 'equal opportunity' for presidential and parliamentary candidates to appear on programmes in the state-owned electronic media are provided in the Minimum Broadcasting Standards, which are included in the Electronic Media Act (1996).

This provides that 'where a programme that is broadcast is in respect to a contender for a public office, then each contender is given equal opportunity on such a programme'. Enforcement of this provision is vested in the Broadcasting Council. However, the Council lacks the capacity to monitor and enforce this provision. It has only an arm's-length oversight role. It may respond to complaints, but as of 17 February it claimed to have received none.

The observations of the group, and analysis of the media monitoring data, indicate that the Uganda Broadcasting Corporation has not lived up to the requirements of the Electronic Media Act.

No formal standards or regulations appear to exist for the print media, other than the relevant sections of the Penal Code. The group was informed that both the *New Vision* and the *Daily Monitor* sought to uphold proper journalistic standards.

The regulatory framework governing media and elections is contained in the Press and Journalists Act (1995), which established the Media Council; the Electronic Media Act (1996) which established the Broadcasting Council and includes the Minimum Broadcasting Standards referred to above; the Electoral Commission Act (1997); and the Uganda Broadcasting Corporation Act (2005), which consolidated UTV and Radio Uganda as Uganda Broadcasting Corporation (UBC TV and UBC Radio).

Guidelines

There were no enforceable codes of conduct or guidelines. On 1 December 2005 the Electoral Commission issued a code of conduct in the form of Campaign Guidelines for Presidential Elections, 2006. This provided for equal treatment to be given by the state-owned media to all candidates and their agents. Candidates would enjoy freedom of expression. Provision was made for the imposition of penalties, but the code of conduct has not been enacted.

On 4 January 2006, the Electoral Commission issued Campaign Guidelines for Parliamentary Elections, 2006. These stated that candidates should not be denied reasonable access to and use of state-owned communication media. It did not make provision for penalties.

Media freedom

Uganda enjoys plural media and the airwaves have been liberalised. Freedom of expression, including freedom of the press and other media, is guaranteed under the Constitution. Uganda's print and broadcast media represent a range of political viewpoints and allegiances, and for the most part appear able to present the free expression of these viewpoints.

However, there have been some exceptions. Radio station KFM was temporarily closed in August 2005 because of an alleged breach of the Minimum Broadcasting Standards. The same station was jammed from 24 to 26 February 2006 after it broadcast independent vote tallies. Access to the website of KFM and the Daily Monitor was blocked on 24 and 25 February.

Sections 36–40 of the Penal Code, CAP 120 of the Laws of Uganda, restrict the publication, sale and distribution of publications which, on the discretion of the Minister, are injurious to public interest.

Human Rights Watch and the Uganda Human Rights Commission have alleged government intimidation of the media during the arrest and trial of the FDC presidential candidate. They documented a government directive issued on 23 November 2005, banning media outlets from running stories on him on the basis that this might prejudice his trial. The press largely ignored the ban.[48]

Background

Newspapers in Uganda account for combined daily sales of about 100,000, with an estimated total readership (owing to multiple users for each copy) of about 1.5 million, or about 5 per cent of the population.[49] In contrast, an estimated 64 per cent of the population rely primarily on the electronic media (largely radio), while 34 per cent rely on word of mouth.[50]

Television

Uganda Broadcasting Corporation Television (UBC TV) is a state-controlled commercial television service. Formerly Uganda Television (UTV), it was merged with Radio Uganda in 2005 to form the Uganda Broadcasting Corporation. It broadcasts mainly in English, but also in Swahili and Luganda. UBC covers a radius of 320km from Kampala. Wavah Broadcasting Service (WBS TV) is a privately owned commercial TV station. WBS TV covers an area of 120km centred on Kampala. It also broadcasts, or is planning to broadcast in Jinja, Masaka, Mbarara and Mbale. There are also regional television stations and interest-driven broadcasters where religious programming is prominent.

Radio

The liberalisation of the airwaves provided for the establishment of many private, commercial and community radio stations, mainly on the FM waveband. The state-owned radio service is UBC Radio, operating five stations nationwide. There are also about 100 privately owned radio stations across the country. The group was informed that about one in four of these have a link to a political party, one in six to a religious organisation and one in eight to an ethnic group. Some 46 per cent of advertising revenues are derived from government or parastatal sources.[51]

The group was informed that many radio stations are owned by known government officials, political party members, sympathisers or candidates, some of whom contested the 2006 elections. This enabled them to promote their policies on their radio stations.

Print media

The *New Vision* is a daily newspaper founded in 1986. Originally entirely government-owned under the Ministry of Information, it was listed for privatisation in November 2004. The government remains the majority shareholder, with 80 per cent of the newspaper's shares held by the Ministry of Finance. Its English language circulation is about 35,000 (Monday to Saturday) and 37,000 (Sunday). There is also a Luganda language edition, Bukedde.

The *Daily Monitor* is a privately owned daily founded in 1992, publishing in English. Its circulation is 32,000 (Monday to Saturday), 33,000 (Sunday). The product portfolio of Monitor Publications Ltd also includes 93.3 K FM. The paper claims to be 'free from the influence of government, shareholders or any political allegiance'.

Commonwealth Observer Group report

Solomon Islands Election, 2006

Note: *Some 453 candidates filed nominations in respect of the parliamentary elections. A candidate for one constituency was returned unopposed. Thirteen political parties contested the elections, some political parties claiming the same candidates. Only three registered voters in a constituency are required to sponsor the nomination of a candidate.*

Media

The Solomon Islands enjoys a free and robust media, which played a critical role throughout the election period, including in raising awareness about the election preparations, process and procedures. The media also highlighted the many challenging issues facing citizens in their first post-crisis[52] national parliamentary elections.

During the period in which Commonwealth observers were present in the Solomon Islands, we received the impression that the media took its role and responsibility to the nation seriously and carried out its task of reporting the elections with fairness, objectivity and impartiality. We received no complaints and saw no evidence of media bias or perceived bias towards any individual political party or candidate during the election campaign. We met with representatives of print and electronic media during our consultations.

All media organisations in the Solomon Islands are members of the Media Association of Solomon Islands (MASI). The association is working on a Code of Practice for Media in the Solomon Islands. The code is a voluntary charter to balance the rights and responsibilities of the Solomon Islands media in a free and democratic society. It upholds both the rights of the individual and the public's right to know. It takes into account the traditional values of the Solomon Islands way of life and the duty to hold public institutions to account, consistent with freedom of expression and the public interest in exposing corruption and malpractice.

Print media

The print media comprises two main newspapers – the daily *Solomon Star* and the bi-weekly *National Express*. Both are published in English. There are no newspapers in Pijin.

The *Solomon Star* is privately owned by a pioneer Solomon Islands journalist. It is published in Honiara from Monday to Friday. More than 60 per cent of the average daily circulation of 5,000 copies is sold in the capital, while the rest are distributed only in those provincial urban centres to which a daily flight is available.

Unreliable air transportation has prevented newspapers from being flown to most of the provinces. Prior to the recent crisis, the newspaper was widely circulated in all provinces. However, the tension has caused planes to stop flying to many places, resulting in the drop in circulation to most parts of the country. *Solomon Star* management say the situation is slowly returning to normalcy. During the period of the elections, the Solomon Star circulation jumped to an average daily circulation of 7,000 copies.

The *Solomon Star* covered the elections extensively in the weeks leading up to and throughout polling and counting of votes. Its news stories and commentaries made strong references to the need for clean elections.

The *National Express* published little political advertising except for news and commentary on the elections. The newspaper is printed in Fiji and air freighted back to the Solomon Islands for distribution.

The Electoral Commission used the print media, especially the *Solomon Star*, to educate the voters about the elections. In the lead-up to polling day, the Commission published full-page advertisements in the newspapers explaining to voters the various steps for voting and giving voters an update on the preparations for the elections. Election advertising in the media continued even up to the day of polling as there is no law preventing this from happening.

Electronic media

There are no local television stations. Satellite TV is available at hotels and to those who can afford it. There is no local content on such stations.

There are two radio stations in the Solomon Islands: the government-owned Solomon Islands Broadcasting Corporation (SIBC) and the commercial FM radio station, Paoa FM, which is owned by the *Solomon Star*.

SIBC is established under the Broadcasting Corporation Ordinance of 1976. The law stipulates that the government provides an annual grant to the corporation on an annual basis. It also empowers SIBC to accept and broadcast advertisements to supplement its budget.

SIBC is heard in nearly all parts of the Solomon Islands and is a 24-hour service. The Electoral Commission used SIBC on a daily basis to inform voters about the election process and preparations.

The Commission had to pay for its use of radio, just like any other organisation throughout the election period. No political party, individual or group received free airtime to advertise election material on SIBC.

SIBC reported extensively on the campaign and preparations for the elections on its news and current affairs programmes on a daily basis. In the lead-up to polling day and counting of votes, SIBC reporters were sent to various provinces to report on the conduct of polling and the results of counting. They sent regular daily reports, which kept listeners throughout the nation up to date on the progress of the polls and the counting of votes and the eventual declaration of results.

Paoa FM, a radio station which targets youth, also provided 'user pays' airtime for election advertising, though few candidates or parties made use of this facility.

6 Conclusion

From the outset and throughout the arguments in this book, the central role of the media in the democratic arena has been established and re-emphasised. Free expression – bringing news, publishing, disseminating or merely sharing it without interference or other barriers – is a fundamental human right. Therefore the media has a great role to play, and an even greater responsibility to bear.

As argued in the *Handbook for European Union Election Observation* (2008, p. 54), freedom of expression is an integral part of a democracy. Regional organisations such as the African Union, the Caribbean Community, the European Union, the Pacific Islands Forum and the Association of Southeast Asian Nations all advocate a place for freedom of expression, and it is already guaranteed in the laws of most developing countries. The next step for the developing countries is to ensure that these guarantees are actually enforced and respected.

The testimonies of individual journalists and reports from Commonwealth Observer Groups reinforce the challenges (and opportunities) faced by the media in covering elections. A strand in common is that they see the media to be the 'eyes and ears' of the community – to the extent that freedom of the media is critical to whether or not observers declare an election to be credible.

To reiterate, *The Danish Democracy Canon* argument demands that people be informed of what is happening in their surroundings, that they make up their minds on how they will benefit from and improve the community, and that the communities find the best-placed person amongst them to further those interests. These dynamics can only be met if the media is fulfilling its role as a professional and independent conveyor of news.

In 2005, the Commonwealth Press Union (CPU) said:

Elections are a key area where the print media can help civil society understand its rights. These are about making choices, providing a direct say in the way a country is run and affirming the involvement of every member of the electorate in the democratic process. Such choices cannot be made unless the electorate has sufficient knowledge of the issues and personalities involved, and an understanding of the situation in which the country finds itself. For the press to help in the process requires professional, responsible, unbiased people-centred journalism. The dissemination of such information is a key task of the press in any democracy, and one that assumes greater importance in emerging democracies where the concept of simply casting a vote can be a novel experience. The implications of voting have also to be explained in an accessible and user-friendly way'.[53]

To fulfil this mandate, the media should:

- Live by the standards and codes of its profession, negotiated amongst themselves and, where possible, negotiated with regulators. This must include banishing the practices of: taking 'transport money' or 'brown envelopes' – synonyms for bribery – from political players; writing about events in a biased way; or undertaking work for a political party of a politician (for whatever gain, including financial).

- Understand the legal environment in which they operate. The media should know the legal framework that governs the elections it is covering, and should be able to interpret these quickly if required.

- Ensure that its own place in society is guaranteed by legislation and campaign against any actions that may limit its work.

- Follow technological change and innovation closely, because changing technologies offer both challenges and opportunities for the media. Only the technologically savvy can expect to reap the full fruits of innovation. The tools a news reporter used to cover elections in 1991 have been completely transformed in less than two decades, and these are evolving rapidly. Taking advantage could reduce costs and lead to better access. This point is reinforced by Jacky Sutton, who says (in the context of Iraq) that new media can dilute the influence of partisan 'old media' institutions. Across the region, developments in information technology have meant that communication tools are in the hands of increasingly heterogeneous constituencies, so have expanded the public space. This has undermined monopoly by the elite of the flow of information and has created an expectation of public dissent, necessary for any meaningful pluralist politics.[54]

- Be brave enough to take on the challenges required to safeguard democracy, but also understand that no story is big enough to die for.

Lastly, we conclude by reaffirming the guidelines drawn by the Commonwealth Broadcasting Association for the Commonwealth Secretariat:

- Establish a specialist Elections Unit (even if it comprises just one individual)

- Train your election team and ensure that an experienced senior journalist leads your team; and finally

- Establish an overall election programme plan: what programmes will be produced? What formats will be used? What rules will apply to programmes involving rival candidates? How will the programmes help to promote democracy? How will the issues be explained? Communicate this plan to the electoral body, to the politicians and to the audience.

Appendix 1: Commonwealth Observer Group Reports

In the foregoing chapters, selected reports of Commonwealth Observer Groups (COGs) are used to illustrate the media's place in democracy. The examples focus on those segments of the reports that deal with the media.

The Commonwealth Secretariat asks observers to 'report on the credibility of the electoral process, whether the conditions exist for a free expression of will by the electors and if the election results are credible'. Each group's report also contains practical recommendations to help improve election arrangements for the future. Part of the observers' mandate is explained below:

The 'election event' should not be seen in isolation: the Commonwealth therefore views the election in the context of the democratic process as a whole. Observers are concerned with the integrity of key processes that affect the election but begin well beforehand, and the Secretariat sees election observation as dovetailing with work to strengthen these processes well before and after the election. The observer group has to act impartially and independently and shall conduct itself according to the standards expressed in the International Declaration of Principles to which the Commonwealth is a signatory. It has no executive role; its function is not to supervise, but to observe the process as a whole and to form a judgement accordingly. In its Final Report, the group is also free to propose to the authorities concerned recommendations for change on institutional, procedural and other matters as would assist the holding of future elections.[55]

The COG reports are important to the extent that, first, they have a chapter or section specifically dedicated to the functioning of the media and, second, they outline specific recommendations to improve the environment, which the Commonwealth Secretariat doggedly follows up with governments to ensure a high rate of implementation.

The reports are honest in their assessment of the environment in which the media operates during an election, and the issues they raise will sound familiar to many readers. If a reader finds that a report, however low-key in tone, offers examples of situations they have dealt with in their own environment or that they seek to overcome, then its inclusion in this book is worthwhile.[56]

References and Bibliography

Article 19 (1998) *Election Reporting: A practical guide to media monitoring.* London: Article 19.

Article 19 (1994) *Guidelines on Election Broadcasting in Transitional Democracies.* London: Article 19.

Article 19 (2005) *Guidelines for Election Broadcasting.* London: Article 19.

Burnheim, Sally (1999) 'The Right to Communicate: The Internet in Africa'. London: Article 19. See: http://www.article19.org [accessed 14 January 2009]

Commonwealth Broadcasting Association for Commonwealth Secretariat (2001) *Commonwealth Election Broadcasting Guidelines.* London: Commonwealth Broadcasting Association for Commonwealth Secretariat.

Commonwealth Press Union (2001) *Elections and Election Reporting.* London: Commonwealth Press Union.

Denmark Ministry of Education (2008) *The Danish Democracy Canon.* Copenhagen: Denmark Ministry of Education.

Epstein, Edward J (1966) *Inquest: The Warren Commission and the Establishment of Truth.* New York: Viking.

European Commission (2008) *Compendium of International Standards for Elections* (second edition). Brussels: European Commission.

European Commission (2008) *Handbook for European Union Election Observation* (second edition). Brussels: European Commission.

Forau, Peter (2006) Pacific Islands Forum statement. Suva, Fiji, 13 April 2006. Unpublished.

Freedom of Expression Institute (1999) Malawi court orders fair election coverage, *http://www.fxi.org.za/pages/Publications/Medialaw/fairelect. htm* [accessed 21 January 2009].

Gutmann, Amy (1987) *Democratic Education.* Princeton: University Press.

Guynn, Jessica (2007) 'Growing Internet role in election: Videos, fundraising among many uses candidates employ'. San Francisco Chronicle, 4 June 2007. Available at: *http://www.sfgate.com/cgibin/ article.cgi?f=/c/a/2007/06/04/BUGI6Q5L181.DTL* [accessed 14 January 2009]

Hatuse, Ryuei (2002) 'Foundation of an Interstate System in East Africa'. *Hiroshima Peace Science* 24.

Howard, Ross (2004) *Media and Elections: An Elections Reporting Handbook.* Institute of Media, Policy and Civil Society. See: http:// portal.unesco.org/ci/en/files/18541/11304302341media_elections_ en.pdf/media_elections_en.pdf [accessed 21 January 2009]

Human Rights Watch (2006) In Hope and Fear: Uganda's Presidential and Parliamentary Polls. Human Rights Watch Briefing Paper. New York and London: Human Rights Watch.

International Federation of Journalists (2004) *Elections Reporting Handbook.* IFJ: http://www.i-m-s.dk/files/publications/Media%20and%20Elections%20handbook%202004%20pdf.pdf [accessed 21 January 2009].

Lallana, Dr Emmanuel C. (undated) *SMS and Democratic Governance in the Philippines.* See: http://www.apdip.net/projects/e-government/capblg/casestudies/Philippines-Lallana.pdf, [accessed 21 January 2009].

Lange, Yasha, and Andrew Palmer (eds) (1995) *Media and elections: A handbook.* Produced by the European Institute for Media. Brussels: Tacis.

Little, John (2008) 'The fourth power and the rise of yellow journalism'. Available at: *http://www.opednews.com/maxwrite/print_friendly.php?p=THE-FOURTH-POWER-AND-THE-R-by-John-Little-080916-777.html* [accessed 14 January 2009]

Pertierra, R et al. (2005) *Mobile Phones, Identity and Discursive Intimacy. Human Technology: an Interdisciplinary Journal on Humans in ICT Environments*, Volume 1 (1), April 2005, pp. 23–44.

Pertierra, R et al. (2002) *TXT-ING Selves: Cellphones and Philippine Modernity.* Manila: De La Salle University Press.

Posada-Carbo, Eduardo (1996) *Elections Before Democracy: The History of Elections in Europe and Latin America.* Institute of Latin American Studies Series. New York: St. Martin's Press.

Schnellinger, Lisa (2001) *Free & Fair: A Journalist's Guide to Improved Election Reporting in Emerging Democracies.* Washington DC: International Center for Journalists.

Society for Environmental and Human Development (1995) *Handbook on Election Reporting: Tips, background and relevant information to help cover the Parliamentary Elections.* Bangladesh: Society for Environmental and Human Development (SEHD).

Stanford Encyclopedia of Philosophy (2007) 'Civic Education'. Available at: *www.science.uva.nl/~seop/entries/civic-education* [accessed 14 January 2008]

United Nations Education, Scientific and Cultural Organization (2005) '2005 Elections in Iraq: Briefing Notes'. Paris: UNESCO.

UNESCO (2005) *A Reporter's Guide to Election Coverage.* Paris: United Nations Education, Scientific and Cultural Organization (UNESCO).

United Nations: *Universal Declaration on Human Rights.* Available at: *http://www.un.org/Overview/rights.html* [accessed 14 January 2009]

Winkler, Matthew and David Wilson (1998) *The Bloomberg Way – A Guide for Reporters and Editors* (pp. 9–10, 234–236). New York: Bloomberg.

Other Sources

International Federation of Journalists Declaration of Principles on the Conduct of Journalists. See *http://www.ifj.org/en/articles/ifj-declaration-of-principles-on-the-conduct-of-journalists* [accessed 4 February 2009]

National media code of conduct for Guyana. See: *http://www.anfrel.org/resources/others/mediacodeofconduct.pdf* [accessed 21 January 2009]

National media code of conduct for Zimbabwe. See: *http://www.journalism.co.za/index.php?option=com_content&task=view&id=224&Itemid=205* [accessed 21 January 2009]

National media code of conduct for Tanzania. See: *http://www.kas.de/proj/home/pub/82/2/year-2005/dokument_id-8959/index.html* [accessed 21 January 2009]

Available at *http://www.thecommonwealth.org/* [accessed 14 January 2009]:

Commonwealth Observer Group to Zimbabwe elections, 2000

Commonwealth Observer Group to Zambia elections, 2006

Commonwealth Observer Group to Solomon Islands elections, 2007

Commonwealth Observer Group to Kenya, 2007

Commonwealth Observer Group to Sri Lanka elections, 2005

Commonwealth Observer Group to Guyana elections, 2006

Commonwealth Observer Group to Malawi elections, 2004

Commonwealth Observer Group to Guyana elections, 2006

Council of Europe Committee of Ministers Recommendation R(99)15. See: *https://wcd.coe.int/com.instranet.InstraServlet?command=com.instranet.CmdBlobGet&InstranetImage=538369&SecMode=1&DocId=409946&Usage=2*

International IDEA, Code of Conduct: Political Parties Campaigning in Democratic Elections. See: *http://www.idea.int/publications/coc_campaigning/index.cfm* [accessed 21 January 2009]

ACE Electoral Knowledge Network. Media and Elections. Available at: *http://aceproject.org/ace-en/topics/me* [accessed 14 January 2009]

Country reports by Daniel Nyirenda (Malawi), Joyce Mulama (Kenya), Timothy Selemani (Kingdown of Swaziland), Anthony Everett Fraser (Trinidad and Tobago), Milton Walker (Jamaica), Irene !Hoaes (Namibia) and Makereta Komai (Fiji Islands).

Internet resources

www.Aceproject.org

http://www.techterms.com/definition/media

http://www.guardian.co.uk/media/pda/2008/jun/10/futureofjournalismhowthei

http://gretawire.foxnews.com/2008/08/18/is-the-washington-post-unfair-in-its-election-coverage/all-comments/

*http://www.articlearchives.com/government-public-administration/
    elections-politics/1505625-1.html*

http://www.rsf.org/article.php3?id_article=24913

*http://www.eci.gov.in/CurrentElections/ECI_Instructions/ins_goa_30040
    7.pdf*

http://www.answers.com/topic/exit-poll

http://www.washingtonpost.com/wp-dyn/content/article/2008/

http://www.bizcommunity.com/Article/196/66/30597.html

Notes

1　Mark Stevens, Head of Democracy at the Commonwealth Secretariat (personal communication, October 2007).

2　Younger journalists tend to have little experience of covering elections and, in their professional lives, have not been party to the democratisation process.

3　Accessed 18 December 2008.

4　Paragraph 6 of the 'Singapore Declaration of Commonwealth Principles' signed by Commonwealth Heads of Government at a meeting in 1971.

5　*Commonwealth Election Broadcast Guidelines*, 2001.

6　The handbook outlines obligations by the media as well as other stakeholders in the coverage of an election.

7　For the European Commission, these questions are important test cases when determining whether an election is credible.

8　See *http://aceproject.org/ace-en* [accessed 19 December 2008]

9　*Ace Encyclopaedia* is part of the Ace Electoral Knowledge Network that has done significant research in media and elections. Further references can be made at its website at *www.aceproject.org*. Ace is a project of the Electoral Institute of Southern Africa (EISA), Elections Canada, Instituto Federal Electoral – Mexico, Interinational IDEA, International Foundation for Electoral Systems (IFES), the UN Development Programme, the UN Department of Economic and Social Affairs, and the UN Electoral Assistance Division.

10　*The Danish Democracy Canon* discusses media in the context of the four challenges it says that democracy faces. The publication itself is as a result of the Danish government's attempts to list hallmarks in the evolution of the country's democracy.

11　Daniel Nyirenda is deputy editor of the national English-language *Daily Times* newspaper.

12　This and all other reports of Commonwealth Observer Groups in this chapter have been reproduced with the permission of the Commonwealth Secretariat. These groups comprise eminent persons and are usually led by a former president or prime minister, or a very senior politician. Their views are made in their own individual capacities and are not the views of the Secretariat. The Commonwealth Secretary-General provides the government and political parties with copies of the final report in the country where he deployed observers. This forms part of the Commonwealth's commitment to improving the environment for the holding of free and fair elections and improving governance amongst its members.

13　Hatsuse's article was published in the journal *Hiroshima Peace Science* 24 in 2002.

14 The term 'fourth estate' is frequently attributed to the 19th century historian Thomas Carlyle, although he himself seems to have attributed it to Edmund Burke: 'Burke asserts that there were three estates in parliament; but, in the reporters' gallery yonder, there sat a Fourth Estate more important than they all. It is not a figure of speech, or a witty saying; it is a literal fact ... Printing, which comes necessarily out of writing, I say often, is equivalent to democracy: invent writing, democracy is inevitable. ... Whoever can speak, speaking now to the whole nation, becomes a power, a branch of government, with inalienable weight in law-making, in all acts of authority. It matters not what rank he has, what revenues or garnitures: the requisite thing is that he have a tongue which others will listen to; this and nothing more is requisite' (Carlyle, 1905: pp. 349–350).

15 Goldacre's views can be found at: *http://www.guardian.co.uk/ media/pda/2008/jun/10/futureofjournalismhowthei* [accessed 7 January 2009]

16 Jessica Guynn's views appeared in the *San Francisco Chronicle*, where she is a correspondent, on 7 June 2007. The full article can be read at: *http://www.sfgate.com/cgi-bin/article.cgi?f=/c/a/2007/06/04/ BUGI6Q5L181.DTL* [accessed 7 January 2009]

17 Timothy Selemani is a political reporter at the government-owned *Swazi Observer* newspaper.

18 *Handbook for European Union Election Observation* (second edition) (2008), p. 57.

19 Citation can be found at: *http://www.science.uva.nl/~seop/entries/ civic-education/* [accessed 8 January 2009]

20 See: *http://www.articlearchives.com/government-public-administration/ elections-politics/1505625-1.html* [accessed 8 January 2009]

21 After the disputed 2007 elections in Kenya, the Electoral Commission of Kenya announced the result of the presidential ballot only on state broadcaster KBC, fuelling complaints of there being an absence of a fair and level playing field.

22 The ACE Knowledge Network provides examples of countries where a blackout period or a period of reflection is seen as important ahead of an election at: *http://aceproject.org/ace-en/topics/me/ med/med06/med06c/default* [accessed 8 January 2009]

23 Many would argue that this is why paid advertising is an unfair option – both to poor parties that may have a strong message and to the electorate, which is saturated by campaign materials only the rich can afford to broadcast.

24 A memo to a provincial electoral office from the Elections Commission of India is very clear on this. See: *http://www.eci. gov.in/CurrentElections/ECI_Instructions/ins_goa_300407.pdf* [accessed 8 January 2009]

25 Full definition is at NDI website *http://www.accessdemocracy.org/ files/1417_elect_quickcounthdbk_1-30.pdf* [accessed 3 February 2009].

26 Ibid.

27 A according to online dictionary *http://www.answers.com/topic/ exit-poll* [accessed 8 January 2009], an exit poll is a poll taken of a sample of voters as they leave a polling place. Such polls are used especially to predict the outcome of an election or to determine the opinions and characteristics of the candidates' supporters.

28 Anthony Everrett Fraser is a veteran broadcast journalist from Tinidad and Tobago. He has written for the Associated Press news agency and also works for the British Broadcasting Corporation.

29 In an online mail chain, a political party writes a letter in its support and sends it to designated email or postal recipients. The letter asks that the recipient forwards it to others. For example, a chain letter might end with a message like: 'Please forward this letter to 15 people you know'.

30 RSS is a method of syndicating or publishing information on your website through an XML application. This allows other websites or applications to import your RSS feed, which contains the information you are publishing, into their website or application; see Bleepingcomputer.com (*http://www.bleepingcomputer.com/glossary/ definition267.html* [accessed 4 February 2009])

31 Pertierra's article appeared in the journal *Human Technology*. It went on further to explain other important uses of the cellular phone, such as keeping provincial and branch or district officials linked with their headquarters or communicating when candidates should show up at meetings to ensure the maximum exposure to potential voters during the campaigning period.

32 The Sierra Leone case was noted in the report of the Commonwealth Observer Group and in personal communication with Yvonne Chin, a Commonwealth Secretariat official who acted as spokesperson for the group.

33 According to Dr Emmanuel C Lallana in his unpublished paper 'SMS and Democratic Governance in the Philippines'. The paper investigates the various SMS-based services that enhance citizen participation.

34 *Financial Times*, 9 December 2008 at: *http://www.ft.com/cms/ s/0/04a981ce-c553-11dd-b516-000077b07658.html?nclick_check=1* [accessed 9 January 2009]

35 Joyce Mulama is East Africa Bureau Chief for development news agency Inter-Press Service.

36 Helal's comments were carried in a story in the *New York Times* headlined 'For Al Jazeera, Balanced Coverage Frequently Leaves No Side Happy' authored by Samuel Abt (16 February 2004).

37 IRIN mainly covers human-interest stories, especially in locations where the United Nations has programmes.

38 Accessed on 21 January 2009 at *http://ethics.iit.edu/codes/coe/int.federation.journalists.html*

39 Winkler and Wilson (1998) *The Bloomberg Way: A guide for reporters and editors*, p. 234.

40 The International Institute for Democracy and Electoral Assistance (International IDEA) is an intergovernmental organisation that supports sustainable democracy worldwide. Its objective is to strengthen democratic institutions and processes. International IDEA acts as a catalyst for democracy building by providing knowledge resources, expertise and a platform for debate on democracy issues. It works together with policy-makers, donor governments, UN organisations and agencies, regional organisations and others engaged in democracy building.

41 Main sources include the International Federation of Journalists Declaration of Principles on the Conduct of Journalists; national media codes of conduct/guidelines in elections from: Guyana, East Timor, Tanzania, Zimbabwe and South Africa; Commonwealth Election Broadcasting Guidelines; the Council of Europe Committee of Ministers Recommendation R(99)15; Article 19 Guidelines on Election Broadcasting in Transitional Democracies; UN Special Rapporteur on Freedom of Opinion and Expression, Annual Report 1999; International IDEA, *Code of Conduct: Political Parties Campaigning in Democratic Elections*; and *The Bloomberg Way – a Guide for Reporters and Editors*.

42 This meeting and its outcomes was reported by online journal *Bizcommunity*. See: *http://www.bizcommunity.com/Article/196/66/30597.html* [accessed 12 January 2009]

43 Milton Walker was UK Correspondent for Jamaica's *Gleaner/Voice* Group when he wrote this piece.

44 Veteran Fijian journalist Makereta Komai is editor of the Pacific News Agency (PacNews), the only information service with a reach across many of the Pacific island nations.

45 Irene !Hoaes is a journalist at the public broadcaster, the Namibia Broadcasting Corporation. She reports on political and economic issues.

46 Both the Democracy Monitoring Group (DEMGroup) of domestic observers and the European Union (EU) international observers carried out detailed monitoring of the electoral coverage in the print and broadcast media in the run-up to the elections.

47 The UJSC examined whether media coverage from 1–21 February 2006 was positive or negative, considering both the explicit judgement (or bias) of the report, and the subject's framing or context (portrayal).

48 Human Rights Watch: In Hope and Fear: Uganda's Presidential and Parliamentary Polls, Human Rights Watch Briefing Paper, February 2006.

49 Information provided by New Vision.

50 Information provided by Broadcasting Council.

51 Figures provided by Uganda Radio Network.

52 In April 2003, facing a deteriorating domestic situation, Prime Minister Kemakeza requested Australian intervention to provide assistance and restore law and order in the country. In July 2003, military and civilian personnel from Pacific Island Forum member states arrived in the Solomons as part of a Regional Assistance Mission to the Solomon Islands (RAMSI). See: *http://www. thecommonwealth.org/Shared_ASP_Files/UploadedFiles/C4E1 BBD5-676D-490B-B5ED-6C51F43E0BFE_SolomonIslandsCOG Report2006-amalgamated.pdf* [accessed 4 February 2009]

53 Sadly, the CPU ceased to exist at the end of 2008.

54 Sutton's comments are posted at http://www.uniraq.org/news-room/getarticle.asp?ArticleID=814 [accessed 14 January 2009]

55 This is the standard instruction the Secretariat gives to observers, who, although constituted by the Commonwealth Secretary-General, form an independent group and make up their own minds as to whether an election has been credible or not.

56 Detailed background to the work of the Observer Groups and their terms of reference can be found on the Commonwealth Secretariat website at: *www.thecommonwealth.org* [accessed 12 January 2009].

Index